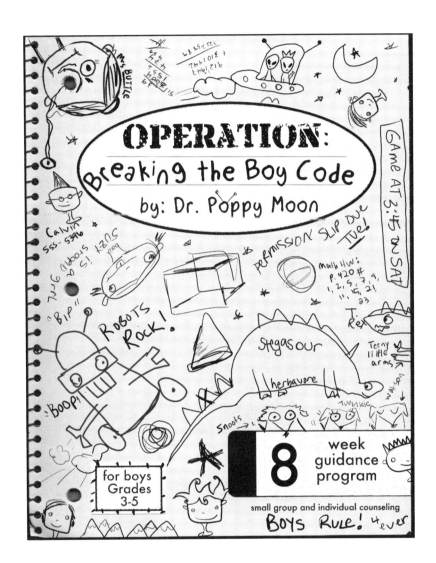

© 2009 by YouthLight, Inc.
Chapin, SC 29036

All rights reserved. Only pages marked "Reproducible" may be copied for student use. No other part of this book may be reproduced or transmitted in any form or by any means, electronic, mechanical, including photocopying, recording, or by any information storage and retrieval system, except in the case of reviews, without the express written permission of the publisher, except where permitted by law.

Edited by Susan Bowman

ISBN—978-1-59850-064-6

Library of Congress Control Number:
2008943804

10 9 8 7 6 5 4 3 2 1
Printed in the United States

PO Box 115 • Chapin, SC 29036
(800) 209-9774 • (803) 345-1070 • Fax (803) 345-0888
yl@youthlightbooks.com • www.youthlightbooks.com

"Whatever you can do, or dream you can, begin it. Boldness has genius, power, and magic in it."

- Johann Wolfgang von Goethe

Acknowledgements

I would like to acknowledge the boys at Myrtlewood Elementary School for inspiring me to create a program that will help young men all over the world.

To my boys: I love your zest for life, your humor, your strengths, and your vulnerabilities. Thank you for letting me into your lives. I hope I have taught you to always find the best in yourself and others. Keep letting your lights shine!

Thanks to my mom and dad, Calvin and Jean Ann Moon, and my husband, Dr. James B. Collier – It was because you believed in me that I believed in myself!

I am forever in debt to Cathy Wooldridge, Martha Roop, and Dr. Brad Willis, three outstanding educators who have always supported me in my "unique" endeavors!

Special recognition goes to my fearless models: Everick Gay, Landon Jacobs, Aaron Jones, Houston Taylor, and Gabriel Van Etten.

Lastly, a very special thanks to Bob and Susan Bowman. I am so thrilled to have found editors who support and encourage my creative process. Who knew that a bit of magic would bring us together?

Dedication

To Watson – the best long dog in the world!

About the Author

 Dr. Poppy Moon has spent most of her adult life thinking about how to help children and adolescents blossom into unique socially and emotionally healthy individuals – and, more importantly, how to teach adults tricks and techniques to assist in this process. It is rare to find Dr. Moon without some kind of puppet, magic trick, role-play costume, or art project geared towards positive child development.

Dr. Moon, a National Board Certified Licensed Professional Counselor and certified school counselor, works as an elementary school counselor and in private practice. She is an adjunct professor at the University of West Alabama. Dr. Moon is a weekly columnist for the Northport Gazette, a monthly columnist for Kids Life Magazine, and is a regular TV guest on Great Day Tuscaloosa.

A dynamic speaker and presenter, Dr. Poppy Moon conducts high-energy, hands-on workshops for counselors, teachers, mental health professionals, and other educators across the nation. She also presents motivational and educational programs to professional adults. She has published several peer-reviewed journal articles in the field of art-related play therapy.

Dr. Moon is married to Dr. James B. Collier, a clinical psychologist. They have three miniature dachshunds, Watson, The Twinkie, and Snoots, and three rather self-important cats, Lulu, The Fuzzy Kitty, and Little Bitty Kitty (who sports a hot pink rhinestone collar).

Table of Contents

Operation Breaking the Boy Code — 1
Understanding Masculinity — 1

How to Use This Book — 3
Operation Breaking the Boy Code Dictionary — 5
BCB Rite of Passage – Initiation — 6
Tips on Selecting Group Members — 7
Operation Breaking the Boy Code Parent Letter — 8
Operation Breaking the Boy Code Permission Slip — 9
Group Member Checklist — 10
Pre-Group Prep — 11
The Magic Counselor Box — 12
The Magic Counselor Box Checklist — 13

Group Oath — 14
Group Oath Signs — 15

Breaking the Boy Code Handbook — 23
Preparing the Boy Code Handbook — 24
    Boy Code Handbook Title Page — 27
    This Book Belongs To — 28
    Our Group Oath — 29

Lesson 1: Our Secret Society—The Boy Code Brotherhood — 31
Objectives — 31
Materials — 31
Copies — 31
Pre-Group Prep — 31
Opening — 32
Activity: Getting to Know You Game — 33
Homework — 33
Follow-up — 33
Evaluation — 34
Individual Counseling — 34

Lesson 1 Worksheets — 35
    Getting to Know You Game — 36
    Our Group Oath — 38
    Secret Handshake Homework — 39
    Super Secret Boy Skills: How to Write a Note with Secret Code — 40

Super Counselor Extension Activities for Lesson 1 — 41
    Extension Activity #1: Oath Flashcards — 42

Lesson 2: Knights of the Round Table — 45

Objectives	45	Activity: A Knight's Tunic	46
Materials	45	Follow-up	46
Copies	45	Evaluation	47
Opening	45	Individual Counseling	47

Lesson 2 Worksheets — 49
- Character Traits — 50
- The Legend of King Arthur and the Knights of the Round Table — 51
- Colors and Their Meanings — 53
- Symbols and Their Meanings — 54
- Super Secret Boy Skills: Be a Super Amazing Mind Reader! — 55
- How to Make a Knight's Tunic — 56

Super Counselor Extension Activities for Lesson 2 — 58
- Extension Activity #1: Personal Shield — 58
- Extension Activity #2: Quick Quote — 62
- Extension Activity #3: Daily Affirmation Bookmarks — 64

Lesson 3: Wisdom of the Tribe — 67

Objectives	67	Activity: Group Totem	68
Materials	67	Follow-up	68
Copies	67	Evaluation	69
Opening	67	Individual Counseling	69

Lesson 3 Worksheets — 71
- The Tribe of the Same — 72
- My Totem Animals — 74
- How to Make a Group Totem — 76
- Super Secret Boy Skills: How to Make a Spinner — 79

Super Counselor Extension Activities for Lesson 3 — 81
- Extension Activity #1: Paper Towel Totems — 81
- Extension Activity #2: Quick Quote — 84

Lesson 4: The League of Extraordinary Heroes (Part 1) — 87

Objectives	87	Follow-up	89
Materials	87	Evaluation	90
Copies	87	Individual Counseling	90
Opening	88	Follow-up	90
Activity: Making a Comic Book Cover	89		

Lesson 4 Worksheets	**91**
Superhero Idea Sheet	92
Me- The Superhero	93
Super Secret Boy Skills: How to Draw a Cartoon Boy	94
My Cartoon Reference Sheet	96
How to Make a Comic Book Cover	97
Super Counselor Extension Activities for Lesson 4	**98**
Extension Activity #1: Personal Heroes	98
Extension Activity #2: Quick Quote	100
Daring Counselor: Superhero Finger Puppets	103

Lesson 5: The League of Extraordinary Heroes (Part 2) — 105

Objectives	105	Follow-up	108
Materials	105	Evaluation	109
Copies	105	Individual Counseling	109
Opening	106	Follow-up	109
Activity: Making a Comic Book	108		

Lesson 5 Worksheets	**111**
Bullying – A Superhero Sized Problem	112
Comic Book Planning Sheet	114
Super Secret Boy Skills: How to Make a Superhero Flip Book	115
How to Make a Comic Strip	117
Comic Book Templates	119
Super Counselor Extension Activities for Lesson 5	**125**
Extension Activity #1: Quick Quote	125
Extension Activity #2: Bully Mad Lib	127
Daring Counselor: Comic Book Role Play	129

Lesson 6: The Way of The Samurai — 131

Objectives	131	Activity: Samurai Mask	132
Materials	131	Follow-up	132
Copies	131	Evaluation	133
Opening	131	Individual Counseling	133

Lesson 6 Worksheets	**135**
The Samurai Virtues	136
The Way of the Warrior	137
Japanese Symbols and Their Meanings	138
Super Secret Boy Skills: Make an Origami Fox	140
How to Make a Samurai Mask	142
Samurai Mask Template	145

Super Counselor Extension Activities for Lesson 6 — **146**
    Extension Activity #1: Quick Quote — 146
    Extension Activity #2: The Way of the Warrior Pledge — 148
    Daring Counselor: Koinobori Flying Fish — 151

Lesson 7: The Magic Circle — 157

Objectives	157	Activity: Making Magic!	159
Materials	157	Follow-up	159
Copies	157	Evaluation	159
Opening	158	Individual Counseling	160

Lesson 7 Worksheets — **161**
    The Magic Circle — 162
    The Magician's Code — 163
    The Ash Trick — 164
    Soda Can Through Table — 166
    The Reversed Card — 168
    Super Secret Boy Skills: Make a Message in Invisible Ink! — 170

Super Counselor Extension Activities for Lesson 7 — **171**
    Extension Activity #1: Quick Quote — 171
    Extension Activity #2: Learning Your Own Trick — 173
    Daring Counselor: Planning and Performing a Magic Show — 174

Lesson 8: Initiation — 175

Objectives	175	Initiation Ceremony	176
Materials	175	Follow-up	183
Copies	175	Evaluation	183
Pre-Group Prep	176	Individual Counseling	183
Opening	176		

Lesson 8 Worksheets — **185**
    Initiation Affirmations — 186
    My Initiation Affirmation to You — 187
    Initiation Secret # 1 — 188
    Initiation Secret # 2 — 189
    Initiation Secret # 3 — 190
    Initiation Secret # 4 — 191
    Initiation Secret # 5 — 192
    Initiation Secret # 6 — 193
    Initiation Secret # 7 — 194
    Initiation Secret # 8 — 195
    Boy Code Brotherhood Certificate — 196
    Boy Code Brotherhood Group Photo — 197

References — 198

Operation: Breaking the Boy Code

Understanding Masculinity:

Historically men have reveled in activities that encouraged camaraderie, cooperation, and the celebration of maleness (Town, 2004). The friendships formed from a lifetime of male bonding forged alliances of loyalty and respect that followed families through centuries. Men earned honor and respect through their actions. Masculinity defined a man who took care of his family, displayed civic responsibility, spoke the truth, kept his word, championed the weak, worked hard, was humble, caring, and recognized his limitations (Franklin, 1984).

Over time, these markers of manhood have shifted from reality into a mythical ideal. The opportunity for boys to learn these qualities from men has changed drastically. Single parent homes, absent fathers, the feminization of early education, and the lack of available male role models leave boys lacking both socially and emotionally (United Nations Development Fund for Women, 2001).

Gender roles are firmly established in our society (Adler, Kless, & Adler, 1992). To keep the status quo, society perpetuates a false male stereotype as the ideal. Males are supposed to be tough, dominant, in total control of themselves, their emotions, and their surroundings. They must be wealthy and have attractive girlfriends. Men must be prepared to fight for their way, even if this involves inflicting emotional or physical violence towards another. To walk away from a fight is social suicide, resulting in an immediate loss of respect from peers. If a boy does not tow the party line, he may be labeled as a freak, queer, homo, or other derogative term (Pollack, 1999).

Boys learn by modeling the behavior of men around them. If they are instructed to regularly suppress emotions "Stop that crying!" or pain "Shake it off!" they will start to think of these normal human experiences as unacceptable or unmanly. Boys who try to discuss personal concerns with other boys or men may be told to "Suck it up" and "Don't be a wimp!" Early on a boy learns that he must not be weak or vulnerable, that internal issues must be solved alone, and that emotions must be repressed (Martino & Meyenn, B., 2001).

Women also assist in promoting society's view of manhood (Kindlon & Thompson, 2000). Mothers may shoo boys out of the kitchen rather than let them assist in "women's work". Sewing and crafts are a girls domain. Mothers may chide boys who show an interest in dolls, fashion, or other activities that are considered traditionally female.

Unfortunately, family, friends, counselors, teachers, and coaches may unwittingly encourage and reward stereotypical behaviors. The jock is exalted for his physical performance, a teen is complimented on his expensive clothes, and a boy is playfully teased because he is the object of many girls' affections. This is hollow praise that does not focus on the inner qualities of a man (Pollack, 1999).

The media assists in firmly cementing this false ideal into the minds of young boys. Rappers, celebrities, and sports figures are regularly shown on TV and in advertisements flaunting wads of cash, expensive "bling" (jewelry, watches, cars), and sexy women (Hust, 2006). These men appear to be devoid of humanistic feelings and enjoy watching others suffer (Media Awareness Network, 2008). For example, Donald Trump, on his show *The Apprentice*, regularly fires competent, educated, hardworking adults over trivial incidents. His firings are cruel and demeaning. Rather than offer constructive criticism, he wields his power like an executioner's blade.

Even cartoons are loaded with gender stereotypes. Research indicates that boys watch approximately 2-4 hours of cartoons daily (Herr, 2007). The male character is usually portrayed as strong, aggressive, and intelligent. There is a major difference in the abilities of the male character when compared to the females or other males of lesser stature (APA, 1997).

Due to extreme external pressure to conform to the masculine ideal, boys begin to doubt the still, small voice that speaks their inner truth. They start to buy into the masculinity myth. Eventually, boys lose the ability to identify and express feelings. Ultimately, boys lose a part of their humanity.

Unfortunately, I have witnessed this happen to several boys I have worked with therapeutically over a long period of time. When the boys are from ages 6-8, they have hopes, dreams, and plans. They believe that the world is basically a good place. These boys love to "help" me push my projector cart to my office or carry my papers, all the while debating whether Spiderman is cooler than Snoots (my miniature dachshund). At the end of the day they rush to hug me before getting on the school bus. The boys hug me so hard that I can almost feel my ribs touch my spine! I hug them back just as hard.

Around the beginning of third grade I start to see subtle, but noticeable changes. Family issues, finances, problems at home, divorce, learning difficulties, and untimely deaths, began to wear on their tiny souls. Academic, social, and behavior problems begin to manifest. If these situations are not adequately addressed, the spark of hope starts to dim. I can actually see a physical tightening of the jaw muscles. They still accept my hugs, but I have to initiate.

I believe that these boys are incredibly frightened, worried, and confused. Since boys are not encouraged to talk about their feelings and concerns, they push that fear deep inside and put on "The Front". The Front is the self-made mask that shows only carefully controlled "normal" reactions. Once The Front is in place, I notice that their jaws square out, their eyes harden, and a cool wariness replaces youthful enthusiasm.

Luckily, all our boys aren't grown up yet! **Operation: Breaking the Boy Code** was created out of the need for an innovative, effective small group guidance program to educate boys about real masculinity. **Breaking the Boy Code** focuses on teaching the importance of emotional health along with life skills and friendship skills. Most importantly, this program celebrates maleness and what it means to be a modern boy.

How to Use This Book

The purpose of **Operation: Breaking the Boy Code** is to help boys in grades 3-5 redefine their view of masculinity, masculine behaviors, and what it means to truly be a man. The goals of the program are simple:

- To increase friendship and communication skills
- To provide the opportunity for boys to experience a diversity of masculinities
- To build self-esteem and self-awareness through a variety of expressive therapy techniques

Operation: Breaking the Boy Code is an 8-week small group counseling curriculum that can be used effectively in schools, boys clubs, scouts, after school programs, community mental health centers, and private practice. Lessons have also been adapted for use in individual therapy sessions.

The book is sectioned into eight lessons, complete with an opener, an activity, group discussion, and a session evaluation. Most lessons will fit into a 45-60 minute time frame.

Following the main lesson, you will find **SUPER COUNSELOR LESSON EXTENSIONS**, which are additional activities that could be used during a longer group, in additional group sessions, or in individual counseling sessions.

I am also adding a special section in some lessons for **DARING COUNSELORS!** We should all aspire to be daring counselors in our practices. Daring Counselors are not afraid of mess, enjoy the creative art therapy process, and are willing to go the extra mile to reach group members.

At the end of each section, you will find a **Super Secret Boy Skills (SSBS)** handout. These are fun activities that encourage creativity and cognitive processing skills.

You will see my signature cat eye glasses appear with a callout bubble throughout the book. These bubbles contain my favorite tips and tricks that I use in my own practice.

* Ancora Imparo means "I am still learning."
  Well into his eighties, Michelangelo penned this quote into the margin of his sketch book.

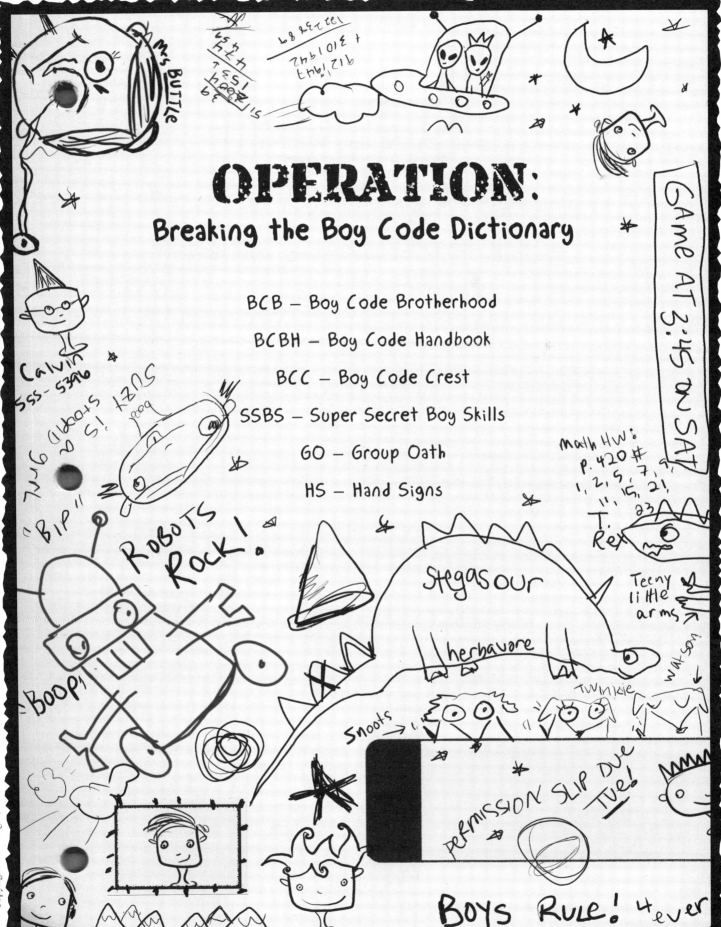

BCB Rite of Passage - Initiation

In researching this book, I found it fascinating how other cultures have well defined rites of passage. These ceremonial rites are not for show, but necessary to the culture itself. A mother mourns losing her little boy on his bat mitzvah, however she joyously celebrates the fact that her son is now a man. Rites of passage are societal boundaries, a logical way to help guide youth from one phase of life to another. Youth who do not have rites of passage experiences often feel lost, since they have no tangible bearings (Hill, 2008). Gang initiation rituals, horrible though they are, actually give youth a sense of purpose. They understand the hierarchy, take pride in working their way up the ladder, and feel confident in the safety of their sacred brotherhood (Hill, 1997).

I have created this program as a rite of passage that ends in initiation into the Boy Club Brotherhood (BCB). As boys work their way through each lesson, they are learning and growing socially, emotionally, and developmentally. The Initiation Ceremony is a special way to reward group members on an emotional, rather than material, level.

The Initiation Ceremony celebrates:

- The completion of an 8 week (or longer) program
- Personal growth
- Social growth
- The work of the group

If you choose to initiate, you will need to make each member a Boy Code Handbook (BCHB). Instructions on how to make the book are included in the next section. At the first session, counselors will give each member their own handbook.

 Each chapter has a section marked by an image of the Boy Code Crest (BCC). This section gives BCB instructions for each lesson.

* **If you do not want to use the initiation ceremony or deal with the handbooks – no worries! Each lesson can easily stand alone with no modifications.**

Tips on Selecting Group Members

I created **Breaking the Boy Code** ideally for groups of 6 to 8 members. The members should be a balance of personalities, from the stereotypical jock, to the introverted nerd, and everyone in between.

Since this program is geared more towards the enrichment of personal and social skills, potential group members with issues that would better be served in individual or family therapy sessions should be excluded.

There is a noticeable difference in the cognitive and emotional development of 3rd grade boys when compared to 4th and 5th graders. For this reason, groups should be composed of all 3rd graders or a mix of 4th and 5th graders.

Boys can be referred to the group by their teacher, parent, counselor, or administrator. The best way to select group members is to ask teachers for names of boys who might be good candidates. Teachers are on the front lines, and they know exactly who would benefit from this program. Administrators are also a good source, however many of the boys they refer could be potential behavior problems!

When placing members in groups, be sure you do not bring together members who will be detrimental to each other. These combinations might include:

- A bully who has victimized one particular boy for years and the victim himself
- Boys of different races who maliciously and deliberately provoke each other
- Boys of extremely high socioeconomic status and boys of low socioeconomic status

The main goal is to create a group where "members will work together optimally" (MacLennan & Dies, 1992). A good mix of boys will find a working equilibrium that encourages the shy member, quietens the loudmouth, and ensures that all members voices are heard.

OPERATION:
Breaking the Boy Code

To the parent/guardian of: _____ :

This letter is to inform you that I will soon be starting a group in which I would like for your son to participate in. The group is called **Operation: Breaking the Boy Code**. The purpose of **Breaking the Boy Code** is to help boys in grades 3-5 redefine their view of masculinity, masculine behaviors, and what it means to truly be a man. The goals of the program are simple:

- To increase friendship and communication skills

- To provide the opportunity for boys to experience a diversity of masculinities

- To build self-esteem and self-awareness through a variety of expressive therapy techniques

I hope that you will allow your son to participate in this unique opportunity! If you have any questions, please do not hesitate to call me _____ at _____ . Please sign and return the attached permission slip below by _____ .

OPERATION:
Breaking the Boy Code

Permission Slip

I give my son, _____ , permission to participate in the **Breaking the Boy Code** group.

Parent/Guardian Name (please print)
_____

Parent/Guardian Signature
_____

Contact Information:

(w): _____

(h): _____

Group Member Checklist

Member Name	Parent Contact Info	Returned Permission Slip	Other Info

Pre-Group Prep

Before your groups begin, you will want to complete the pre-group prep checklist. This does not include pre-lesson preparations, which are located near the beginning of each lesson.

	Collect signed permission slips
	Locate a space suitable for group meetings. Ideally, you will want to find a space that: • Allows for confidentiality • Is large enough to give all members space to work on group activities • Has a safe storage area for group artwork, the large group oath, and hand signs • Has a whiteboard or chalkboard
	Put together your Magic Counselor Box (see checklist p.13)
	Make a large poster of the Group Oath (GO) to hang in group room (p.14)
	Make a poster with the GO Hand Signs (HS) to hang in group room (p. 15-22)
	Create a Boy Code Handbook for each member (p.23-29)

The Magic Counselor Box

The Magic Counselor Box is your portable kit that contains different types of materials that you will usually need for sessions. Your box could be a simple tub with a lid. Or, if you are the creative type, you could decorate an old suitcase with wheels, spray paint a big box with star stencils – let your inner artist be your guide! Here are two great examples:

The Magic Counselor Box Checklist:

	Aluminum foil		Newspaper
	Awl – **counselor use only!**		Old fabric
	Box cutter – **counselor use only!**		Old magazines
	Brad fasteners		Pencils, pens
	Brown paper bags		Pipe cleaners (all colors)
	Cardstock – white and colored		Popsicle sticks
	Colored embroidery floss		Poster board
	Colored Pencils		Rulers
	Colored Yarn		Scissors (get good scissors that can actually cut!)
	Construction paper		Stapler
	Crayons		Tape – Clear, scotch, blue painter's, and duct tape
	Embroidery needles		Tissue paper
	Glue Sticks		Trash Bags
	1 hole punch		White paper plates
	3 hole punch		White school glue
	Low temp glue gun		Wrapping paper – all styles. Metallic designs are great for shields and other shiny projects (check for these after the holiday season!)
	Low temp glue gun sticks		Yardsticks
	Magic Embellishments: Glue on jewels, glitter, sparkles, stickers, beads, shiny paper, shells, google eyes, colored stamp pads and rubber stamps – basically anything that is fun and can accent art projects (just browse around your local art/hobby shop)		And everything else but the kitchen sink!
	Markers		

Group Oath

"A real man is **r**espectful, **e**mpathetic, **a**ttentive, **l**oyal, **m**entally strong, **ac**tive, and **n**oble.

He is **respectful** when he shows concern for others.

He is **empathetic** when he tries to understand the feelings of others.

He is **attentive** when he is watchful of his situation.

He is **loyal** when he shows faithfulness to his family, friends, and his beliefs.

He is **mentally strong** when he thinks clearly and avoids drugs and alcohol.

He strives to be **active** and physically fit.

He is **noble** when he is courageous, generous, and honest.

I will try to be a real man in all things."

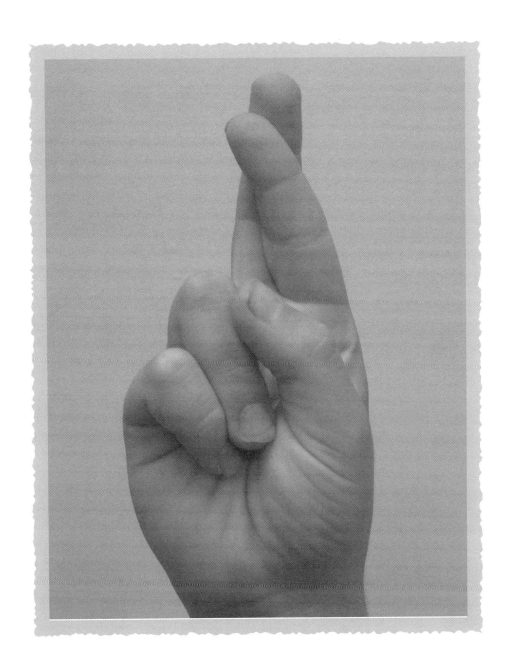

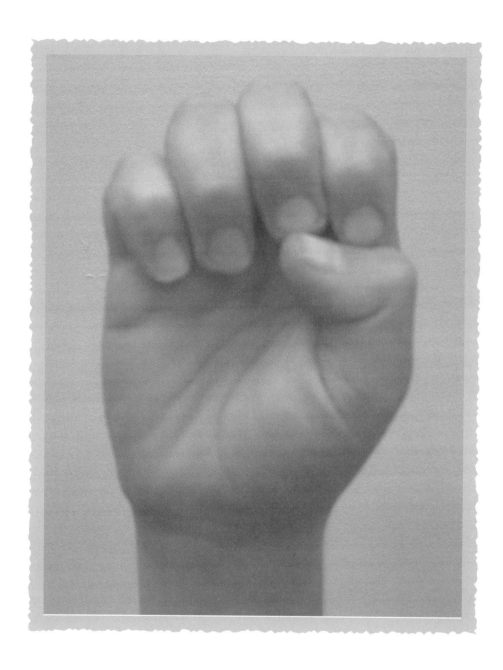

e

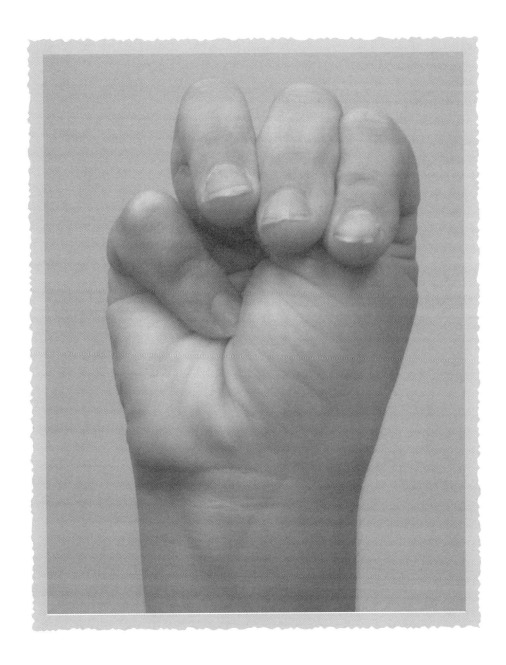

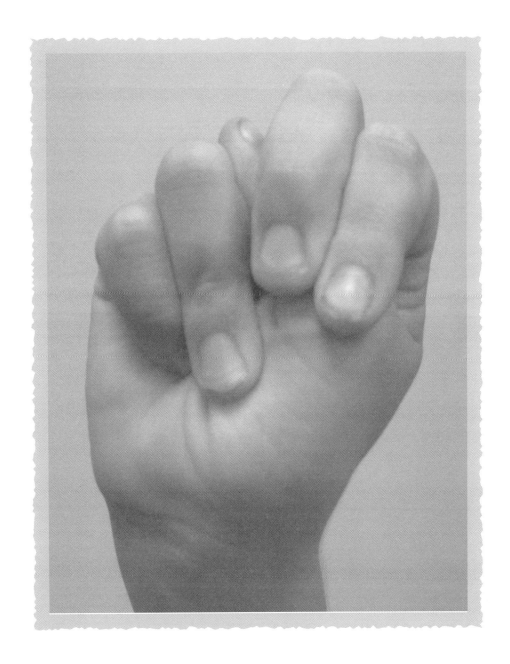

Preparing the Boy Code Handbook

Step 1:

Purchase enough paper folders with 3-prong fasteners for each group member in the same color.

Step 2:

Take the first sheet of the BCBH and cut out the crest and title. Glue them to the front of the folders.

Step 3:

Initially insert the following pages into the book for Lesson 1:
1. Title Page
2. This Book Belongs to
3. Our Group Oath
4. Lesson Pie Chart

You will add pages to the book at each meeting. Here is a list of the pages that will be added for each lesson.

Lesson 2
1. Character Traits
2. The Legend of King Arthur and the Knights of the Round Table
3. Colors and Their Meanings
4. Symbols and Their Meanings
5. Quick Quote (optional)

Lesson 3
1. The Tribe of the Same
2. My Totem Animal
3. Quick Quote (optional)

Lesson 4
1. Superhero Idea Sheet
2. Me – The Superhero
3. Cartoon Reference Sheet
4. My Hero (optional)
5. Quick Quote (optional)

Lesson 5
1. Bullying – A Superhero Sized Problem
2. Comic Book Planning Sheet
3. Comic book page templates
4. Quick Quote (optional)
5. Superhero Mad Lib (optional)

Lesson 6
1. The Samurai Virtues
2. The Way of the Warrior
3. Japanese Symbols and their Meanings
4. Quick Quote (optional)
5. The Way of the Warrior Pledge

Lesson 7
1. The Magic Circle
2. The Magician's Code
3. The Ash Trick
4. Coke Can Through Table
5. The Reversed Card
6. Quick Quote (optional)

Lesson 8
1. My Initiation Affirmation to You
2. Initiation Secrets 1-8
3. Boy Code Certificate
4. Boy Code Group Pic (optional)

Many copiers have a built in hole punch feature. Use it!

Don't put all the pages in the BCHB at once! Let members add them one at a time as they work through lessons (otherwise, members will try to "work ahead" and not focus on the current discussion).

OPERATION:
Breaking the Boy Code Handbook

This Boy Code Handbook Belongs to

_____

Our Group Oath

"A real man is **r**espectful, **e**mpathetic, **a**ttentive, **l**oyal, **m**entally strong, **a**ctive, and **n**oble.

He is **respectful** when he shows concern for others.

He is **empathetic** when he tries to understand the feelings of others.

He is **attentive** when he is watchful of his situation.

He is **loyal** when he shows faithfulness to his family, friends, and his beliefs.

He is **mentally strong** when he thinks clearly and avoids drugs and alcohol.

He strives to be **active** and physically fit.

He is **noble** when he is courageous, generous, and honest.

I will try to be a real man in all things."

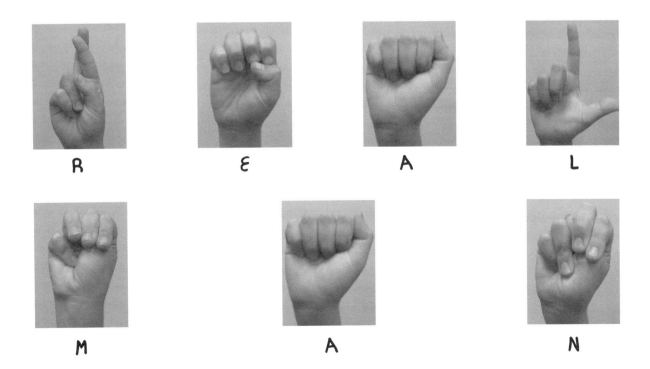

Lesson 1:
Our Secret Society-
The Boy Code Brotherhood

Time: 45-60 minutes

Objectives:

- Boys will understand the purpose of the group
- Boys will meet and learn more about other group members

Materials

- Magic Counselor Box
- Large Group Oath Poster
- Hand Signs Posters
- Container (fishbowl, hat, box)
- 1 Boy Code Brotherhood Handbook for each member (see p. 23)

Copies:

- Getting to Know You Game Cards
- Secret Handshake Homework
- Group Oath
- Super Secret Boy Skill Handout

Pre-Group Prep:

- Cut out the cards, fold, and place in the container.
- Place Oath and Hand Signs on the wall

I like to use seating charts for my groups. This way I can place members in strategic "therapeutic" places. Friends are separated and no one feels left out!

Always make 1 copy per member unless directed otherwise.

Opening

1. Group members sit in a circle. Have members sit by members they do not know well (use a seating chart!).

2. Explain the purpose of the group. Here is a script you can use, however it is better to deliver the information in a casual, chatty style.

Counselor:

I am really excited to see all of you here! You are going to be a part of a group that is going to have a really fun experience. For the next 8 weeks we are going to be hanging out once a week. We are going to talk about what it means to be a real man, someone who is brave, loyal, and true. We will learn about masculinity, feelings, and how to be a friend.

Don't worry, we are not going to just sit around and talk! We will be doing some seriously cool projects – like creating a 6-foot tall totem pole, making a knight's tunic, and turning yourself into a superhero!

Have you ever heard of a secret society? A secret society is a brotherhood of friends who have secret oaths, special hand signs, codes, and secret symbols. This group has all those things and more! Our secret society is called the Boy Code Brotherhood, or BCB.

Today I am going to teach you the secret oath and hand signs. We will recite the oath and use the hand signs at the beginning of each meeting.

Every meeting you will earn a mark in your Boy Code Book. At our eighth session, when you have earned all your marks and your circle is full, you will be initiated into BCB. At initiation, your will learn the meaning of our motto and crest, our secret handshake, secret code words, and some other cool stuff!

If you happen to miss a meeting, you can earn your mark by meeting with me for an individual lesson.

Remember that these secrets are fun secrets. You can tell your family or a trusted adult about them and what they mean. Try not to tell your friends or classmates about them, so you will have something special just between the eight of you!

3. Hand out copies of Our Group Oath. Tell them that this is their own special copy to keep secret in a safe place. Go through the oath and hand signs several times. Use the large posters as a visual reference.

4. Give members their BCHB. You can go through the book with the members, explaining each section. (Keep the books for members between lessons so they do not lose them!)

Activity: Getting to Know You Game

1. Have group members go around the circle and introduce themselves.

2. Determine the youngest member in the group.

3. Show the group the container with the cards. Explain that the container will be passed around the group. Each member will draw a question card and read it to the group. The person to the cardholder's right must answer the question.

4. Give the container to the youngest member. They will draw and read the first card.

5. A group member can pass on a question, however he must immediately answer the next question drawn from the container.

6. Continue play until all group members have answered all questions or until there is 10-15 minutes left in the group.

1. If there is extra time left, group members can decorate the cover of their BCHB.
2. Have members color in Lesson 1 on the pie chart in their handbook.

Homework!

1. Explain that secret societies have special handshakes that members use to identify one another. Demonstrate several potential handshakes to the group.

2. Hand out the Handshake Homework worksheet. Discuss directions with the group.

3. Encourage members to practice Oath and Hand Signs 4 times each day.

Follow-up

- Ask the boys the following questions:
  - How do feel about being selected to be in a group like this?
  - What questions do you have for me about the group?

- Hand out the Super Secret Boy Skills (SSBS) handout

Evaluation

- Observe the body language of the group members –did they seem scared, nervous, excited, or apprehensive?

- Observe the interaction between group members. Is there tension? Do members have an instant scapegoat? Is there an obvious leader? Use this information to create your seating chart for the next session.

- If a member seems reluctant to participate or is uncomfortable around the group; meet with them privately to discuss their problems or concern.

Remember to take down the Oath and Signs at the end of the session. You don't want anyone to "happen upon" the secrets!

Individual Counseling

The game in this lesson can easily be adapted for use with an individual client, especially in an initial session. You will need the container with the **Getting to Know You Game Cards**. Counselor and client take turns drawing cards and asking questions. For extra fun, the client can make up questions for the counselor, and vice versa!

Creating a secret handshake is a special way to build rapport between client and counselor. You can use the **Secret Handshake Homework** worksheet as a guide to fashioning your own unique grip!

What is your favorite game?	What is your favorite food?
What is something you are frightened of?	What is something that makes you laugh?
What is something that is hard for you to do?	What is something you enjoy doing?
What is your favorite book?	Who is your favorite comic book hero?
What is something you are really proud of?	What do you want to accomplish one day?

What is your favorite type of music?	What hurts your feelings?
What really makes you mad?	What is the nicest thing someone has said about you?
What is your favorite subject?	What did you have for breakfast?
Who do you live with?	What place do you most want to visit?
Who do you admire most?	When is your birthday? How old are you?

Our Group Oath

"A real man is **r**espectful, **e**mpathetic, **a**ttentive, **l**oyal, **m**entally strong, **a**ctive, and **n**oble.

He is **respectful** when he shows concern for others.

He is **empathetic** when he tries to understand the feelings of others.

He is **attentive** when he is watchful of his situation.

He is **loyal** when he shows faithfulness to his family, friends, and his beliefs.

He is **mentally strong** when he thinks clearly and avoids drugs and alcohol.

He strives to be **active** and physically fit.

He is **noble** when he is courageous, generous, and honest.

I will try to be a real man in all things."

R

E

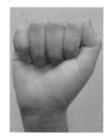
A

L

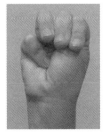
M

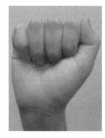
A

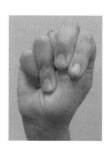
N

Reproducible Lesson 1

Most secret societies have a special handshake that is know only among members. Your job is to create a unique and fun handshake for the group. At the next lesson, all members will show their handshakes and we will choose one to be the Official Group Handshake!

How to Make a Secret Handshake:

1. Brainstorm with another member(s) of the group, an older brother, or any man you respect.

2. Decide how many steps will be in the handshake. 3-5 is a good number.

3. Write out the steps:

    1. High-five up high

    2. High-five down low

    3. High-five in the middle

    4. 1 snap of the fingers

4. Practice makes perfect!

5. Be ready to show your handshake at the next meeting!

How to Write a Note with Secret Code

Step 1:
Make up a secret code with your friends. Here are some secret code ideas.

Reverse the letters of the alphabet:

A=Z, B=Y, C=X, D=W, E=V

Use numbers as letters:

A=1, B=2, C=3, D=4, E=5

Make up your own code! Here is an example. You can complete this code!

Step 2:
Make a secret code key that you keep in a safe place. (You don't want your code to be stolen — especially by a GIRL!)

Step 3:
Start writing! You can even use the secret code to write in a journal or diary!

Solve this code!
7 15 15 4 12 21 3 11

SUPER COUNSELOR EXTENSION ACTIVITIES FOR LESSON 1!

EXTENSION ACTIVITY #1: OATH FLASHCARDS

Materials:

- Copies of the Oath Flashcards
- Glue Sticks
- Scissors
- Index Cards

Activity:

Have group members cut out Oath cards and glue them to the index cards. Use 1 card per sign.

Members can use the cards to help them memorize the parts of the Oath and their corresponding hand signs. They can use the cards to test each other - which is a great way to encourage rapport and bonding!

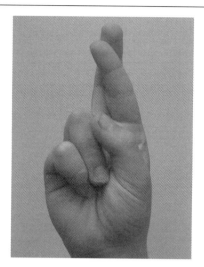

RESPECTUL

A Real Man is **RESPECTFUL** when he shows concern for others.

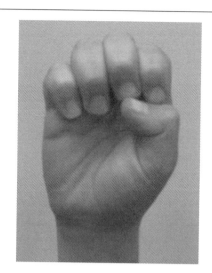

EMPATHETIC

A Real Man is **EMPATHETIC** when he tries to understand the feelings of others.

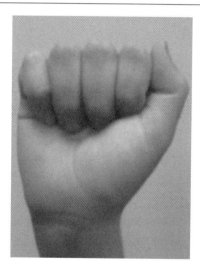

ATTENTIVE

A Real Man is **ATTENTIVE** when he is watchful of his situation.

LOYAL

A Real Man is **LOYAL** when he is faithful to his family, friends, and beliefs.

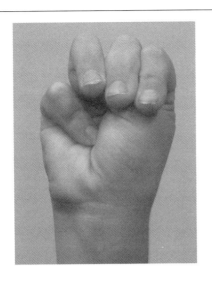

MENTALLY STRONG

A Real Man is
MENTALLY STRONG
when he thinks clearly and
avoids drugs and alcohol.

ACTIVE

A Real Man is
ACTIVE
and
physically fit.

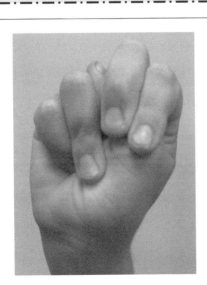

NOBLE

A Real Man is
NOBLE
when he is courageous,
generous, and honest.

Reproducible Lesson 1

Lesson 2:
Knights of the Round Table

Time: 45-60 minutes

Objectives:

- Boys will examine the legend of King Arthur and the Knights of the Round Table, colors, and symbolism
- Boys will discuss characteristics of the King and his Knights
- Boys will create their own knight's tunic

Materials:

- Magic Counselor Box
- Poster of Group Oath and Hand Signs for the wall
- Roll of Butcher Paper or large white paper

Copies:

- Character Traits Handout
- Legend of King Arthur and the Knights of the Round Table
- Colors and Their Meanings
- Symbols and Their Meanings
- SSBS

Opening

1. Group members sit in a circle. Try to have members sit by members they do not know well.
2. Recite Group Oath with secret hand signs.
3. Spend a few minutes sharing potential secret handshakes. Have the group vote on the best handshake.
4. Give out the Character Traits handouts. Pick members to read aloud the character words and definitions one at a time. Give members time to write responses to each word question. Ask members to share what they have written.

5. Group leader reads the Legend of King Arthur and the Knights of the Round Table
6. **Listening Comprehension Questions:**
   - What kind of qualities do you think a king needs to possess?
   - What qualities did King Arthur have?
   - The Knights had courage. What is courage? Why would it be important for a knight to have courage?
   - Do you think King Arthur and the Knights were ever afraid? Why or why not?
   - Can you be brave and afraid at the same time?
   - Why did King Arthur have the Knights sit around a round table?
   - Do even the best of friends have conflicts?
   - We are sitting in a circle. What does that mean about our group?

Activity

A Knight's Tunic

Knights wore heavy armor and helmets that protected their bodies during battle. Individual knights could not be recognized behind their helmets. To solve this problem, knights put a coat of arms on their tunics and shields. The coats of arms was like personal logo, made with colors and symbols that were special to the knight.

a. Hand out the Colors Worksheet.
b. Ask members to read about the colors and their meanings.
c. Hand out and complete the Symbols Worksheet.
d. Use the directions in the "Making a Knight's Tunic" section.

1. Have members place worksheets in their BCBH.
2. Have members color in Lesson 2 on the pie chart in their handbook.

Follow-up

- Ask the boys the following questions:
  - Tell us about your tunic. Tell us why you picked those colors and symbols.
  - What part of the tunic design is most important to you?
  - Explain what you like best about another group member's tunic.

Evaluation

- Observe the attention level of the boys as they discuss King Arthur, Knights, and their shield.

- Observe the body language of the group members while sharing their coat of arms.

- If a member seems reluctant to participate, meet with them privately to discuss their problems or concerns.

Individual Counseling

1. If client is not familiar with the character traits vocabulary, first work on the Character Traits handout together.

2. Client and counselor read the Legend of King Arthur and the Knights of the Round Table together (each read the alternating paragraph)

3. The following questions can be used to stimulate discussion:

    - What kind of qualities do you think a king needs to possess? Which of these qualities do you possess? Which of qualities do you wish you possessed?

    - The Knights had courage. What is courage? Why would it be important for a knight to have courage? Tell me about a time when you felt courageous.

    - Do you think King Arthur and the Knights were ever afraid? Why or why not? Tell me about a time when you were afraid. What happened? How did you deal with your fear?

    - Can you be brave and afraid at the same time? Tell me about a time when you felt scared and brave.

4. The counselor (or client) can select either the Knight's Tunic or the Personal Shield (**Counselor Extension Activity #1**) as the art therapy activity. Or, both activities could be used over 2-3 sessions.

I like doing art therapy activities over several individual sessions. It gives therapy a sense of continuity, allows more time to focus on a theme, and the clients really look forward to the next session!

CHARACTER TRAITS

✵ **BRAVE** – to face a situation with courage

Write about a time when you were brave:

_____

_____

✵ **LOYAL** - to be faithful to one's family, friends, and personal beliefs

Write about a time when you were loyal:

_____

_____

✵ **DIGNITY** – acting in a mannerly way that gains respect

Write about a time when you saw another group member acting with dignity.

_____

_____

✵ **HONOR** – having a good reputation, keeping one's word

Tell the group about someone whose reputation you admire.

_____

_____

THE LEGEND OF KING ARTHUR AND THE KNIGHTS OF THE ROUND TABLE

Long ago King Pendragon, the King of England died. He had not produced an heir, so there was no one in line to become the next king. Merlin, the land's most powerful wizard, decided hold a tournament of strength and skill. The winner of the tournament would become the next king.

Lots of strong men came to the tournament. They bragged to each other about their muscles, how brave they were, and how many men they had beaten in previous games.

Merlin knew that none of these men had the qualities of a good king. Yes, they were physically strong, but they were not strong of heart. They lied about their personal prowess just to seem tough. They did not understand that a true king needed to love his subjects, be willing to listen to their needs, and be courageous when times were hard.

Merlin took a huge sword of the brightest steel and plunged it deep into a stone. He inscribed on the blade in letters of gold, "Whoever pulls this sword from the stone is the rightful king of Britain." (Allen, n.d.) He then bewitched the sword and the stone. His spell ensured that only an individual who was truly brave, caring, and pure of heart could remove the sword.

All of the contestants believed that they could easily pull the sword from the stone. However, their hearts were not loyal and true, and they could not remove it.

Among the contestants at the tournament was Sir Kay, a young knight who was preparing to compete in the games. Sir Kay realized he had forgotten to bring his sword from their lodgings. He asked his younger brother, Arthur, to go back for it. Arthur looked everywhere for the sword, however he could not find it anywhere! Then he spied the Sword in the Stone near the tournament area. Knowing nothing of Merlin and the challenge, he effortlessly pulled the sword from the stone and took it to his brother.

When the crowds saw Arthur return to the tournament grounds with the sword, all the subjects fell to their knees and bowed, recognizing Arthur as the true King of England.

Young Arthur grew up to become a brilliant King. He showed respect for others and himself, he listened to his subjects' problems, and he helped change a nation. King Arthur was aided by his trusty Knights of the Round Table. The Knights were a true brotherhood of noblemen who served their King and country with courage, dignity, and honor. They went on dangerous quests, rescued damsels in distress, and fought for the freedom of their people.

You might ask why the knights sat at a round table. Originally the Knights sat at a rectangular table. Some Knights believed that those who sat at the head of the table were more favored by the King. This caused jealousy among group. To resolve this conflict, wise King Arthur had the Knights sit around a circular table. This made all the Knights equal, because no seat at the table was better than the other.

COLORS AND THEIR MEANINGS

Knights wore heavy armor and helmets that protected their bodies during battle. Individual knights could not be recognized behind their helmets. To solve this problem, knights put their coat of arms on their helmets and shields. The coats of arms were made from personal symbols that were special to the knight.

BLUE
- Truth
- Loyalty
- Youth

SILVER
- Peace
- Serenity

GREEN
- Hope
- Joy
- Love

PURPLE
- Royalty
- Education
- Magic
- Mystery

YELLOW
- Wisdom
- Joy
- Happiness

BROWN
- Genuineness
- Likes Nature
- Orderly

ORANGE
- Vitality
- Endurance

PINK
- Love
- Beauty

BLACK
- Sorrow
- Maturity

WHITE
- Purity
- Cleanliness

- Which 4 colors describe you best? Draw a circle around your top 4 choices.
- Which 2 colors will you use on your Tunic? What made you select the top 2 colors?

Reproducible Lesson 2

SYMBOLS AND THEIR MEANINGS

Bear: Protects family, friends

Horse: Readiness, prepared

Wolf : Hard working

Eagle: Noble, alert, brave

Dragon: Protection

Bull: Brave, generous

Unicorn: Extreme Courage

Camel: Patient

Salamander: Protection

Snake: Wisdom

Bee: Efficient

Owl: Wisdom

Sun: Glory, splendor

Sword: Justice, honor

Heart in Hand: Charity, sincerity, faith

Tree: New life, personal growth

Horseshoe: Good luck

Ship: Explorer

Castle: Safety

Heart: Love for self and others

CIRCLE 2-4 SYMBOLS TO PLACE ON YOUR TUNIC

Reproducible Lesson 2

Be a Super Amazing Mind Reader!

Step 1:	Before you do the trick, get a secret assistant who is in on the trick.
Step 2:	Choose an assistant from your audience (be sure to pick your secret assistant — no one else should know he is your assistant!)
Step 3:	Tell the audience to pick a number.
Step 4:	Leave the room while the audience picks a number.
Step 5:	Have your assistant sit in a chair with his head bending forward. Put your first two fingers on the assistant's temples. Have your assistant pulse his temples until he counts to the chosen number. You will be able to feel his temples pulse with your fingers.
Step 6:	Grandly announce the chosen number and accept your applause!

How to Make a Knights Tunic

Step 1: Cut off about 2 yards of paper off the roll.

Step 2: Lay out the paper flat on the floor

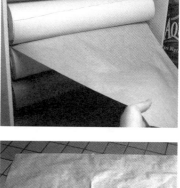

Step 3: Fold the paper in half

Step 4: Using a black marker, draw the neck hole and sides.

Step 5: Cut out the tunic along the lines

Reproducible Lesson 2

Step 6: Using a black marker, draw the coat of arms shape on the front of the tunic

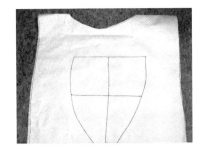

Step 7: Have group members decorate the coat of arms on their tunic.

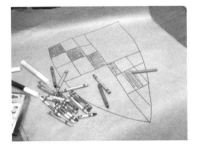

Step 8: Continue decorating until all parts of the coat of arms are complete.

Step 9: Yea! Time to put on your tunic!
You can use yarn or leather string to tie the tunic at the waist.

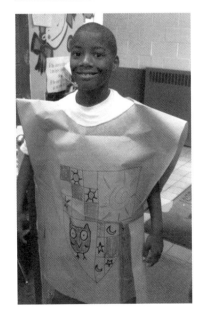

For extra fun, get out the magic embellishments!

Reproducible Lesson 2

SUPER COUNSELOR EXTENSION ACTIVITIES FOR LESSON 2!

EXTENSION ACTIVITY #1: PERSONAL SHIELD

Materials:

- Magic Counselor Box

- Color and Symbol handouts

- 3 Shield Templates - this is a large shield you cut out of poster board or cardboard. Group members lay the shield on their poster board (or cardboard), draw around it with a pencil, and then cut it out.

- White poster board or cardboard

- Kilz spray paint primer (optional)

Most kids need a template or literal example to get started on an art project. Make these up ahead of time so members can see exactly what they are doing!

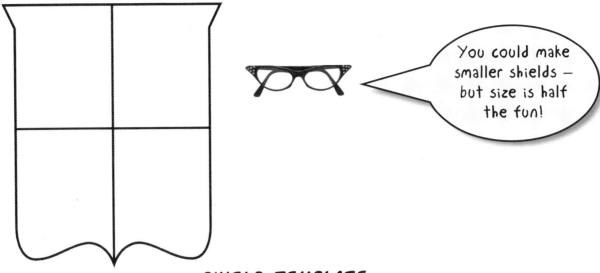

**SHIELD TEMPLATE –
YOUR TEMPLATE SHOULD BE ABOUT 2 ?-3 FEET HIGH
BY 2-2 ? FEET WIDE.**

Pre-Group Prep:

To expedite the activity, you may want to sketch the shield pattern on each member's poster board before the session. If you are using cardboard, go ahead and cut out the shields with the box cutter. If the cardboard has writing or logos on the surface, prime them with Kilz white spray paint primer. Primer is a thick white paint that covers the cardboard and gives you a pure white surface. This is great for coloring over with crayons, markers, and colored pencils.

Activity:

Step 1: Sketch the shield pattern onto the poster board.

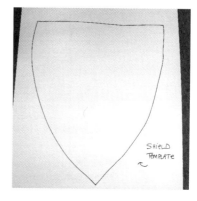

Step 2: Draw the 4 sections

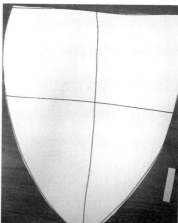

Step 3: Cover the four sections with shiny paper, aluminum foil, colored paper, decorative paper, or color with crayons or markers.

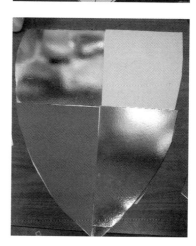

Step 4: Use construction paper to make symbols, attach to each section.

Step 5: Using an awl, scissors, or a sharp pencil, poke 2 holes in the center of the shield. Thread string or pipe cleaners through the holes.

Step 6: Tie the string or wrap the pipe cleaner around the back of the shield, leaving enough room for a handhold.

Step 7: Enjoy! Go off and rescue a damsel in distress or a princess locked in a tower guarded by a horrible dragon!

Extra Fun for Daring Counselors:

Allow group members to paint their shields with acrylic paint. You will need:

- Acrylic paint (in lots of colors – especially metallic gold and silver)
- Brushes
- Clear Gloss Acrylic Sealer
- Plastic sheeting
- Paper plates
- Hair dryer

1. Spread out plastic sheeting over the work area.
2. Have members paint on base coat. Use hairdryer to quickly dry the paint.
3. Paint symbols on cardstock. Embellish! Quick dry symbols using hairdryer.
4. Cut out and glue symbols to the shield.
5. When dry, spray shields with acrylic varnish. This gives them a great glossy sheen!

Extension Activity #2: Quick Quote

Materials:

- Copies of the Quote Worksheet
- Pens or pencils

Quote:

"He that walks with wise men will be wise." - King Solomon

Reproducible Lesson 2

QUICK QUOTE

"He that walks with wise men will be wise." - King Solomon

- Write this quote in your own words. You can ask group members for help!

  _____
  _____
  _____
  _____

- List 4 characteristics of a wise man.

  _____
  _____
  _____
  _____

- Who is a wise man in your life? Why do you look up to him?

  _____
  _____
  _____
  _____

- What 3 things can you do to become wiser in the next year?

  _____
  _____
  _____
  _____

EXTENSION ACTIVITY #3: DAILY AFFIRMATION BOOKMARKS

Materials:

- Magic Counselor Box

- Copies of bookmark worksheet (if you can, print them on white cardstock – they will last longer!)

Activity:

Have clients cut out and color bookmarks. There is also a sheet with blank bookmarks. Group members can use materials from the Magic Counselor Box to make their own creations!

Reproducible Lesson 2

Lesson 3: Wisdom of the Tribe

Time: 45-60 minutes

Objectives:

- Boys will discuss Native American tribes and the importance of individual traits.
- Boys will learn about totem animals and their characteristics
- Boys will create their own group totem pole

Materials:

- Magic Counselor Box
- Poster of Group Oath and Hand Signs for the wall

Copies:

- The Wisdom of the Tribe
- My Totem Animal
- SSBS

Opening

- Group members sit in a circle. Try to have members sit by members they do not know well.
- Recite Group Oath with secret hand signs.

1. Here is a sample script to start the session:

Counselor:

Long ago, before the United States was a nation, Native American Indians lived in this land. Native Americans lived in tribes, which were groups of families and friends who lived, hunted, and worked together to survive. In order for a tribe to be successful, all the members needed to have different skills. Some members needed to be good hunters; others needed to make weapons, while others needed to be planters. They needed members who could sew animal skins, cook corn cakes, and tend to the sick.

These stories were passed down from generation to generation. The stories were important because they reminded the tribe to celebrate, respect and honor the differences of each member.

Here is one such story: (read the Tribe of the Same)

2. Listening Comprehension Questions:

   - What did the young Indians learn from their experience?
   - Why did the young men not listen to the elders?
   - What happened because all the members were the same?
   - What would life be like if we were all the same?

Activity

Group Totem

The Indians realized that each individual member's gifts and talents were incredibly important to the success of the tribe. Indians created totem poles carved with animals to celebrate each member and their personal characteristics.

   a. Hand out the My Totem Animals worksheet

   b. As a group, examine each totem animal and his characteristics.

   c. Have members complete the sections labeled "I am most like _____ when I _____ ."

   d. Ask members to select one animal that they relate to the most.

   e. Use the directions on the Making a Group Totem worksheet

   1. Have members place worksheets in their BCBH.
   2. Have members color in Lesson 3 on the pie chart in their handbook.

Follow-up

- Ask the boys the following questions:
  - Tell us about your animal. What made you select your particular animal?
  - What do you find interesting about another member's animal choice.
  - What does our totem say about the group as a whole?

Evaluation

- Observe the attention level of the boys as they listen and discuss **The Tribe of the Same**

- Observe the personal totem animals each member selected. Does the totem accurately portray the individual?

- Observe members comments on the group totem.

- If a member seems reluctant to participate, meet with them privately to discuss their problems or concerns.

Individual Counseling

Time: 50 minutes

1. Client and counselor read The Tribe of the Same together (each read the alternating paragraph)

2. The following questions can be used to stimulate discussion:

3. What is the moral of the story?

4. What personal qualities and talents would you give to a group?

5. What would life be like if we were all the same

6. Using the **My Totem Animals** worksheet, the counselor and client can go through each animal and discuss the characteristics. The counselor can assist the client in exploring how he personally relates to each totem animal.

7. Have the client select 4-5 personal totem animals. The client can use these animals to make a Paper Towel Totem (instructions are given in **SUPER COUNSELOR EXTENSION ACTIVITY 1**).

Follow-up

Time: 5-10 minutes

- Tell me about your totem animals. What made you select your particular animals?

- If you had to select one animal to represent you, which animal would you choose and why?

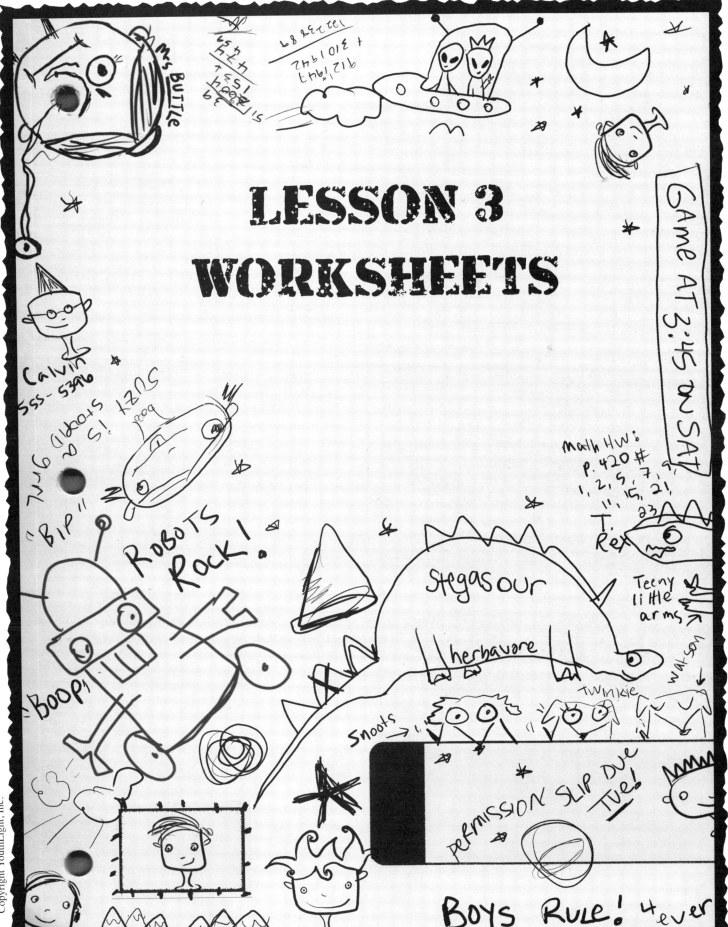

The Tribe of the Same

Once upon a time there was a tribe of Indians. In the tribe was a group of strong young hunters. They liked to brag to each other about their muscles and how clever they were on the hunt. They would tease the other young men who had skills in other areas, such as spear making, weaving, and pottery. "Those things are for sissies! A real man is a hunter!"

The tribal elders called a meeting with the boys. One elder spoke, "It is good that you are young, strong hunters. The tribe needs such members. However, a tribe cannot exist without members who have different gifts. For example, if the earth had no rain, there would be no corn. If there was no fire, there would be no bread. All things are necessary for harmony in life."

The young men talked among themselves. "What do the old men know? We will go off and form our own tribe. A tribe of hunters! We will hunt buffalo and eat like kings!" So the next day the young men packed their bags and took off to form their own tribe.

After several days, the hunters had eaten all their dried meat and fruit. They decided to go together and track a buffalo. "I will bring back the largest buffalo", one of the members said. "Ha!" said another, "It will be me who takes the largest buffalo!" On and on the conversation went, with each member promising to bring in the largest kill.

The tribe realized that they had forgotten to pack their spears. "No matter," said one of the young men. "We will use sticks as spears to kill our prey!"

The tribe walked through the plains, searching for a beast. Soon they found a large buffalo munching grass in the field. Each member ran as quickly as they could towards the animal. When they were in range, each of them threw their sticks at the buffalo with all their might. The sticks hit the buffalo, bounced off and fell to the ground. The buffalo looked irritated, however he continued to munch on the grass.

The young Indians didn't know what to do! Then two of the men tried to push the buffalo in the direction of their camp. The buffalo merely flicked his tail, and continued to eat. Another member grabbed a handful of grass and used it to lure the buffalo down the hill towards their tepees. Much to their surprise, the buffalo followed, eating the grass out of the Indian's hand.

When they reached the camp, the hunters danced and whooped around the beast! "Ah! We will feast on buffalo tonight!" "So, who will prepare the buffalo for dinner?" one asked. The others looked confused. "We are all hunters," one man said. "We do not know how to make a knife to skin the buffalo." "Well," another member said, "even if we did know how to skin it, we don't know how to collect herbs to season it, nor do we know how to make a pot to cook it in!" The conversation continued well into the night. The buffalo, growing tired of the Indians, wandered off into the darkness.

Realizing the error in their plans, the young Indians fell asleep to the sound of their rumbling bellies.

The next day the Indians returned to their tribe, tired and hungry. The elders welcomed them with open arms. After the young men had eaten their fill, one of the elders asked, "So, what have you learned from your experience?"

My Totem Animals

Eagle

Eagle is known for his intelligence, spirit, and risk-taking.

I am most like eagle when I:

study and do well on tests and when I go for the goal in soccer.

Bear

Bear is known for his courage, great strength, and instinct.

I am most like bear when I:

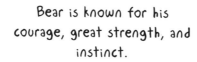

Coyote

Coyote is known for his humor, ability to recognize mistakes, cleverness, and wit.

I am most like coyote when I:

Deer

Deer is known for his compassion, caring, and peace-making.

I am most like deer when I:

Raccoon

Raccoon is known for his curiosity.

I am most like raccoon when I:

Turtle

Turtle is known for his protection of others.

I am most like turtle when I:

Reproducible Lesson 3

Falcon

Falcon is known for his leadership and adventurous spirit.

I am most like falcon when I:

Bat

Bat is known for his ability to keep secrets and his listening skills.

I am most like bat when I:

Owl

Owl is known for his wisdom and insight.

I am most like owl when I:

Lion

Lion is known for his love of family and energy.

I am most like lion when I:

Fish

Fish is known for his quickness.

I am most like fish when I:

Dragonfly

Dragonfly is known for his imagination and goal setting.

I am most like dragonfly when I:

How to Make a Group Totem

Step 1: Cut poster board in half

Step 2: Draw totem animal on the poster board and outline with black marker. Members can refer to the Totem Animals sheet for design ideas, or they can sketch their own animal.

Step 3: Outline, color and cut out totem animal

Step 4: Have group members personalize their artwork with their name

Step 5: Use double-sided tape to affix individual animals to the wall.

Step 6: Stack animals on top of each other.

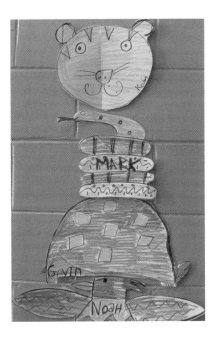

Reproducible Lesson 3

Step 7: Enjoy your group totem!

How to Make a Spinner

You will need:
Paper
Scissors
Your Brain

Horizontal

Vertical

Step 1:	Get a piece of notebook paper or copy paper. Fold the paper in half horizontally.	
Step 2:	Cut down the center of the crease. You now have 2 rectangles.	
Step 3:	Fold each rectangle in half vertically (they will become long and skinny)	
Step 4:	Fold the left hand side bottom corner up to form a triangle.	

79 Reproducible Lesson 3

Step 5: Do the same with the opposite corner.

Step 6: Place one of the rectangles (#1) on a table with the triangles facing up.

Step 7: Place the other rectangle (#2) on top of #1 with the triangles up. #2 should be placed horizontally between the triangles of #1.

Step 8: Fold one of the bottom rectangles to the center.

Step 9: Fold the triangle to the left to the center (it will be on top of the first triangle).

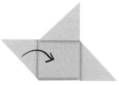

Step 10: Fold the next triangle to the left to the center (it will be on top of the first and second triangle).

Step 11: Fold the last triangle to the center and tuck it under the bottom triangle.

Put it on the ground and spin like a top!
Tip: The tighter the creases, the better the spinner!
You can decorate your spinner with markers, crayons, or colored pencils!

Reproducible Lesson 3

SUPER COUNSELOR EXTENSION ACTIVITIES FOR LESSON 3!

EXTENSION ACTIVITY #1: PAPER TOWEL TOTEMS

Materials:

- Magic Counselor Box
- Empty paper towel or wrapping paper rolls

Safety Alert! Don't use old toilet paper rolls — they may have bacteria on the surface!

How to Make a Paper Towel Totem

Step 1: Cut paper towel roll to desired height.

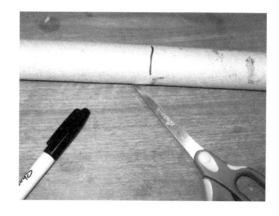

Step 2: Cut slits on the bottom of the paper towel roll. Cut 2 pieces of cardstock approx. the same size.

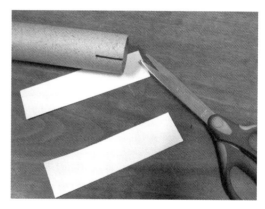

Step 3: Using the cardstock, create a base for the totem.

Step 4: Cut out individual totem animals.

Step 5: Affix individual animals to totem with tape or glue.

Step 6: Enjoy!

EXTENSION ACTIVITY #2: QUICK QUOTE

Materials:

- Copies of the Quote Worksheet
- Pens or pencils

Quote:

"Diversity is the one true thing we have in common. Celebrate it every day." – Anonymous

QUICK QUOTE

"Diversity is the one true thing we have in common. Celebrate it every day." –
Anonymous

- Write this quote in your own words. You can ask group members for help!

  _____
  _____
  _____
  _____
  _____
  _____
  _____

- Pick a group member. Name two ways you are alike.

  _____
  _____

- Pick a different group member. Name 2 ways in which you are different.

  _____
  _____

- Do we always celebrate the diversity in others? Explain.

  _____
  _____

- How could you celebrate the diversity in others this week? List 2 ways:

  _____
  _____
  _____

Make it a goal to celebrate the diversity in others and yourself this week!

Reproducible Lesson 3

Lesson 4:
The League of Extraordinary Heroes (Part 1)

Time: 45-60 minutes

Objectives:

- Boys will investigate the meaning of the word hero
- Boys will discuss the characteristics of heroes and superheroes
- Boys will create their own personal superhero

Materials:

- Magic Counselor Box
- Poster of Group Oath and Hand Signs for the wall
- Piece of long paper tacked to the wall and a marker (or a whiteboard/chalkboard if possible!)
- Examples of Comic Book Covers

Copies:

- Superhero Idea Sheet
- Me-The Superhero
- SSBS

Opening

- Group members sit in a circle. Try to have members sit by members they do not know well.

- Recite Group Oath with secret hand signs.

Here is a sample script to start the session:

Counselor:

How do you define a hero? (write down responses on the paper or whiteboard – be sure they are not talking about superheroes).

I am going say several statements about heroes. I want you to tell me if you agree or disagree with the statement and we will discuss your answers.

- **A hero is courageous and strong.**
- **A hero is never scared or afraid of a situation.**
- **A hero always tries to help others, even if the situation is dangerous.**
- **A hero never cries.**
- **Heroes never get angry.**
- **Heroes are brave.**
- **Heroes are liked by everyone.**

Give me some examples of heroes you know in your everyday life. How are they heroes?

What is the difference between heroes and superheroes?

Answers:

- **Superheroes have extraordinary powers or abilities, however they do not have to be supernatural – like the ability to fly. Batman does not have special powers, but he is a master of martial arts.**
- **A superhero has a strong moral code. He will risk his life for what he believes is right.**
- **He helps people in need.**
- **He does not expect a reward or recognition for his work.**

Activity: Making a Comic Book Cover

If time is limited, you may want to break this activity into 2 lessons. In the first lesson you can complete steps 1-2, and in the second lesson complete step 3 and the Follow-up section.

1. Hand out the **SUPERHERO IDEA SHEET**. Brainstorm with the group and have them write down their answers.

2. Hand out the **ME - THE SUPERHERO WORKSHEET**. Give members time to complete the worksheet. They can refer to the Colors and Symbols Meaning worksheets from Lesson 2 as a reference.

3. Use the directions in the **MAKING A COMIC BOOK COVER** section.

1. Have members place worksheets in their BCBH.
2. Have members color in Lesson 4 on the pie chart in their handbook.

Follow-up

- Ask the boys the following questions:
    - Tell us about your superhero. What were your reasons for selecting:
        - Your colors
        - Your powers
        - Your name
    - What do you find interesting about another member's superhero?
    - How could your superhero work with another member's superhero to fight crime?

Take up the comic book covers at the end of the session. You will use them in the next session's activity.

Evaluation

- Observe the attention level of the boys as they listen and discuss heroes and superheroes.

- Observe the superhero each member selected. Does the superhero have qualities the member personally lacks?

- Observe members' comments on their superhero.

- If a member seems reluctant to participate, meet with them privately to discuss their problems or concerns.

Individual Counseling

Time: 50 minutes

1. Client and counselor discuss the meanings of hero and superhero.

2. Using the **ME - THE SUPERHERO** worksheet, the counselor and client can go through and discuss each section.

3. Use the directions in the **HOW TO MAKE A COMIC BOOK COVER** section.

Follow-up

Time: 5-10 minutes

- Tell me about your superhero.

- What qualities/values/characteristics does your superhero have that you also have?

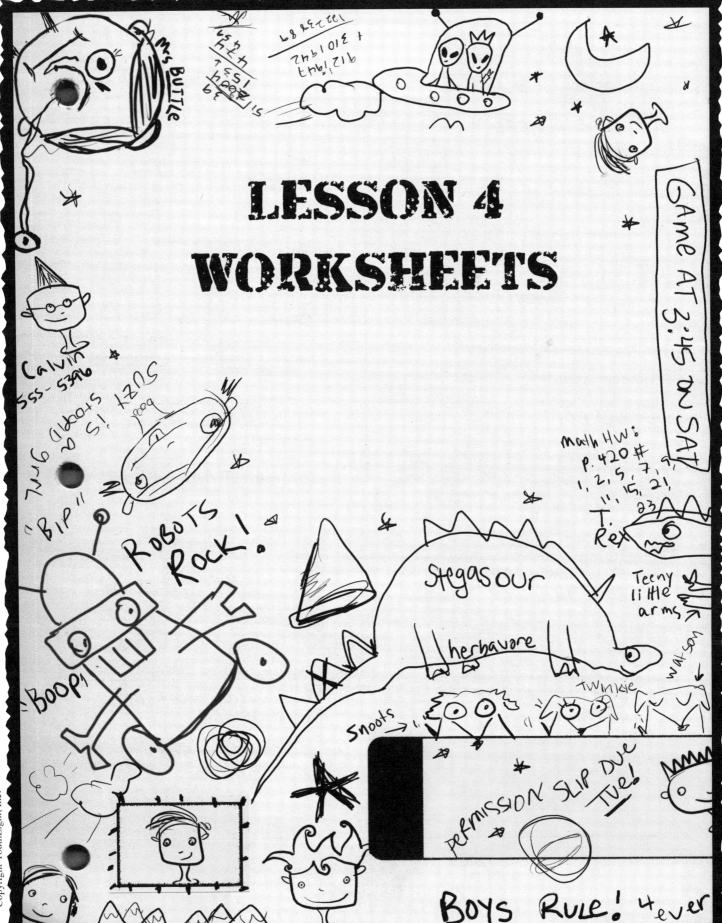

SUPERHERO IDEA SHEET

SUPERPOWERS	• FLIGHT • POWER TO FREEZE ENEMY
COSTUME	• MASK • CAPE
SYMBOL	• SUPERMAN'S "S" SYMBOL • BATMAN'S BAT SYMBOL
SIDEKICK (CAN BE A PERSON OR AN ANIMAL)	• BATMAN'S ROBIN
HOW HE BECAME A SUPERHERO	• SPIDERMAN - BITTEN BY A SPIDER • SUPERMAN - BORN WITH POWERS

ME - THE SUPERHERO!

WHAT IS YOUR SUPERHERO'S NAME?	
HOW OR WHY DID YOU BECOME A SUPERHERO?	
WHAT ARE YOUR SUPERHERO'S SPECIAL POWERS?	
WHAT IS YOUR SYMBOL?	
WHAT ARE YOUR COLORS?	
WHAT KIND OF EVIL DO YOU FIGHT?	
DO YOU HAVE A SIDEKICK? IF SO, IS IT A HUMAN OR ANIMAL? HOW DOES HE HELP YOU?	
DOES YOUR SUPERHERO HAVE A SPECIAL VEHICLE? IF SO, WHAT CAN IT DO?	
WHAT IS YOUR SUPERHERO'S "CATCH PHRASE"?	
WHO ARE YOUR SUPERHERO'S MAIN ENEMIES? WHY?	

Reproducible Lesson 4

HOW TO DRAW A CARTOON BOY

You will need:
Paper
Pencil with an Eraser
Your Brain

Step 1: Start by drawing a head (a large U shape), on a cone shaped body.

Step 2: Give the character hair, eyes, ears, and a nose

Reproducible Lesson 4

Step 3: Add sleeves and shorts.

Step 4: Add arms and legs

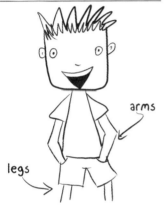

Step 5: Add shoes.

Step 6: Customize your character with designs on his shirt, shoes, shorts, etc. Give him some color with colored pencils!

MY CARTOON REFERENCE SHEET

Cartoons are made of simple shapes. Use this guide when creating new cartoon characters!

Hair

Eyes

Ears

Noses

Mouths

HOW TO MAKE A COMIC BOOK COVER

Step 1: Select a bright piece of construction paper. Cut a piece of white cardstock that is slightly smaller than the construction paper. Glue the white paper to the construction paper.

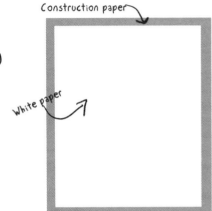

Step 2: Write the name of the character over the top of the white paper, using dramatic, comic book style font.

Step 3: Sketch and color your superhero in a superhero pose (flying, standing at the ready, etc.)

Step 4: Enjoy!

SUPER COUNSELOR EXTENSION ACTIVITIES FOR LESSON 4!

EXTENSION ACTIVITY #1: PERSONAL HEROES

Materials:

- Magic Counselor Box
- Copies of the My Hero worksheet

Reproducible Lesson 4

MY HERO

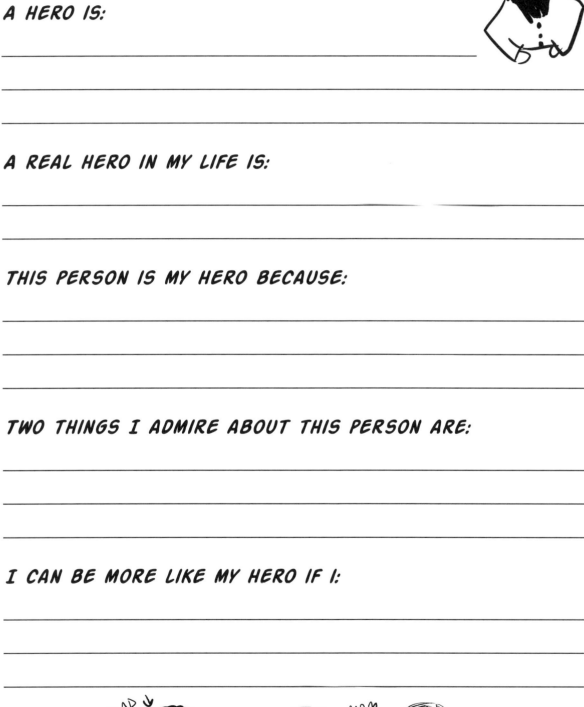

A HERO IS:
_____
_____
_____

A REAL HERO IN MY LIFE IS:
_____
_____

THIS PERSON IS MY HERO BECAUSE:
_____
_____
_____

TWO THINGS I ADMIRE ABOUT THIS PERSON ARE:
_____
_____
_____

I CAN BE MORE LIKE MY HERO IF I:
_____
_____
_____

EXTENSION ACTIVITY #2: QUICK QUOTE

Materials:

- Copies of the Quote Worksheet
- Pens or pencils

Quote:

"You don't have to be a fantastic hero to do certain things -- to compete. You can be just an ordinary chap, sufficiently motivated to reach challenging goals."
– E. Hillary

QUICK QUOTE

"You don't have to be a fantastic hero to do certain things. You can be just an ordinary boy, sufficiently motivated to reach challenging goals."
– E. Hillary

- Write this quote in your own words. You can ask group members for help!

  _____
  _____
  _____

- What are 3 personal goals you have right now?

  _____
  _____
  _____

- Let's plan 2 steps you can do in the next week to help reach each of these goals:

Goal 1:   1.

            2.

Goal 2:   1.

            2.

Goal 3:   1.

            2.

Quick Quote Follow-Up:

1. Last week we talked about personal goals. You wrote out three goals and brainstormed several steps you could take towards these goals during the past week.

- Were you able to follow up on all the goals? Explain.

    _____
    _____
    _____

- Which goals are most important to you?

    _____
    _____
    _____

- If you did not follow through on your goals, should you give up or keep trying?

    _____
    _____
    _____

- Why must goals be broken into many smaller parts?

    _____
    _____
    _____

- How could another group member help you remember to follow through on your goals each week?

    _____
    _____
    _____

SUPERHERO FINGER PUPPETS

Finger puppets are fun to make and can be used constructively in a group setting. Puppets can be used for role-play, which is a great technique to help group members learn new skills and behaviors.

Materials:

- Magic Counselor Box
- Felt in a variety of colors

Activity:

Step 1: Place 2 pieces of felt together. Using a marker, draw the pattern on the felt.

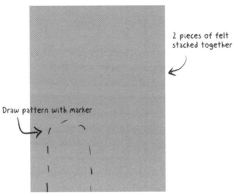

Reproducible Lesson 4

Step 2: Cut out the pattern while you are holding both pieces of felt together.

Step 3: Using a low temp glue gun, apply a strip of glue around the edge of one of the pieces of felt. Remember — don't put glue on the bottom of the puppet!

Step 4: Lay the 2nd piece of felt on top of the 1st, gluing the sides together. Allow the puppet to cool.

Step 5: Using the glue gun, add embellishments to your finger puppets. You can use bits of felt and cloth to make clothing, capes, masks, etc.

Step 6: Insert finger and enjoy!

Lesson 5:
The League of Extraordinary heroes (Part 2)

Time: 45-60 minutes

Objectives:

- Boys will discuss bullying and it's effects
- Boys will develop their own superhero comic book related to bullying.
- Boys will examine each member's book and discuss personal meaning

Materials:

- Magic Counselor Box
- Poster of Group Oath and Hand Signs for the wall
- Piece of long paper tacked to the wall and a marker (or a whiteboard/chalkboard if possible!)
- The **COMIC BOOK COVERS** made in Lesson 4

Copies:

- **BULLYING - A SUPERHERO SIZED PROBLEM!**
- Comic Book Planning Sheet
- Comic Book Page Templates
- SSBS

Opening

- Group members sit in a circle. Try to have members sit by members they do not know well.

- Recite Group Oath with secret hand signs.

Here is a sample script to start the session:

Counselor:

In the last session, we created your own personal superhero. This week we will bring your superhero to life in your own comic book! In the book, your character is going to face a problem that is pretty common these days. The problem is bullying.

Bullying is a problem that most boys face, however they are too embarrassed or scared to talk about it.

You can use the ***BULLYING - A SUPERHERO SIZED PROBLEM*** worksheet to help members focus (especially if you have members with attention problems!).

Let's start off by defining bullying. What is your definition of bullying? (As members brainstorm, write their ideas on the whiteboard)

Bullying is when an individual hurts another on purpose in order to gain power over them.

There are two types of bullying: physical and verbal.

What are some examples of physical bullying? (As members brainstorm, write their ideas on the whiteboard)

Examples: pushing, hitting, shoving, threatening to hurt another, stealing or ruining personal belongings, forcing someone to do something he does not want to do

What are some examples of verbal bullying? (As members brainstorm, write their ideas on the whiteboard)

Examples: name calling, teasing, insulting, spreading lies or rumors

Why do you think bullies act the way they do? (As members brainstorm, write their ideas on the whiteboard)

Examples: to feel powerful, to look cool, to feel important, to feel better about themselves, a way to get attention

A target is someone who is being bullied. What do you think are some characteristics of a target? (As members brainstorm, write their ideas on the whiteboard).

Examples: someone who is small, someone who is large, a person with a disability, someone who is a different race or religion, someone without a lot of friends who is a loner, someone who will not stand up for themselves, someone who gets upset easily

Can someone be a target and not have these characteristics? (yes, anyone can be bullied, and there may not be any real reason the bully picked him)

How do bullies make a target feel inside? (As members brainstorm, write their ideas on the whiteboard).

Examples: sad, lonely, afraid, depressed

How can you avoid being a target?
- Get a buddy – stick up for each other!
- Don't go places where the bully will be.
- Leave situations when a bully arrives.

Have you ever been bullied? How did you deal with it?

Why do you think boys don't like to talk about being bullied?

How can you deal with a bully? (As members brainstorm, write their ideas on the whiteboard).
1. Ignore
2. Walk away
3. Don't show that you are upset; that is what the bully wants! (you can cry alone later, or punch a pillow!)
4. Act confident! Tell the bully in a firm voice to leave you alone.
5. Use the ***MENTAL SUPERHERO SHIELD TECHNIQUE***. When you are being bullied, pretend that you have an invisible shield around your body. Imagine that the taunts and insults hit the shield and bounce off – without hitting you!
6. Use Humor: "You are exactly right! I do wear glasses, so I have four eyes! You have AMAZING counting skills!
7. Agree with the Bully: "Yes, that is your opinion."
8. Get your friends to stick up for you (and do the same for them).
    - Ex: "Back off Steve! No one wants to hear your trash talk!"
9. Don't go to places where the bully hangs out.
10. Get an adult to help!

What is a bystander? (Someone who is around when someone else is being bullied. A bystander may or may not participate in the bullying.)
- Tell me about a time when you were a bystander?
- Did you help the bullied?
- Were you afraid to help because you might get bullied?

How could a bystander be a hero?
Examples:
- Refusing to join in with the bully.
- Try to diffuse the situation: "Ok, John, that's enough. Leave Ron alone."
- Help someone who has been bullied (help them up off the ground, pick up their things, etc.)
- Talk to the target privately; encourage them to talk to an adult.
- If possible, go get a parent, teacher, counselor, or other trusted adult to help.

Activity: Making a Comic Book

1. Hand out the **COMIC BOOK PLANNING SHEET**. Brainstorm with the group and have them write down their answers.

2. Use the directions in the **MAKING A COMIC BOOK** section.

1. Have members place worksheets in their BCBH.
2. Have members color in Lesson 4 on the pie chart in their handbook.

Follow-up

- Ask the boys the following questions:
    - Tell us about your comic. How did your superhero deal with Bullytor?
    - What do you find interesting about another member's comic?
    - How could your superhero work with another member's superhero to fight Bullytor?
    - Would your solutions work in real life?

Evaluation

- Observe the attention level of the boys as the group discusses bullying.

- Note any members who seem uncomfortable with the topic. You may want to discuss the issue with them in private.

- Observe members' comments about bullying and being bullied.

- If a member seems reluctant to participate, meet with them privately to discuss their problems or concerns.

Individual Counseling

Time: 50 minutes

1. Use the counselor script in the Opening section to start a discussion about bullying.

2. Using the **COMIC BOOK PLANNING** sheet, help the client plan his comic book.

3. Use the directions in the **HOW TO MAKE A COMIC STRIP** section.

Follow-up

Time: 5-10 minutes

- Tell me how your superhero dealt with Bullytor.

- Tell me about a time when you dealt with a bully.

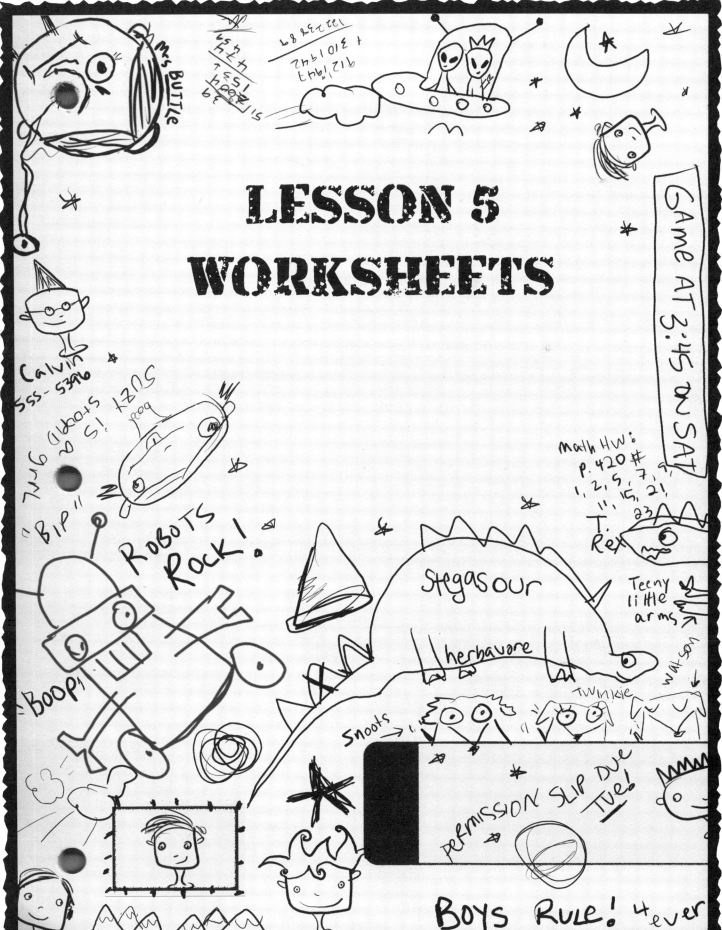

BULLYING - A SUPERHERO SIZED PROBLEM

BULLYTOR!

Bullying is when a person _____ another on _____ in order to gain _____ over them.

The two types of bullying are _____ and _____ .

Physical Bullying	Verbal Bullying
•	•
•	•
•	•
A target is someone who is being _____ .	Examples of a target are: • • •

Bullies can make a target feel:

•

•

•

Reproducible Lesson 5

3 ways to avoid being a target include:

-
-
-

SUPERBOY

10 ways to deal with a bully:

1.	2.
3.	4.
5.	6.
7.	8.
9.	10.

A bystander is someone who
_____
_____ .

A bystander can be a hero if he:
_____
_____

How can the members of this group help stop bullying?

COMIC BOOK PLANNING SHEET

THE PROBLEM:
- THE VILLAIN BULLYTOR HAS ESCAPED FROM PRISON.
- HE HAS TARGETED YOUR SUPERHERO!
- YOU ARE NOW BEING BULLIED!

HOW WILL YOU DEAL WITH BULLYTOR USING 3 REAL LIFE TECHNIQUES WE DISCUSSED?

HOW WILL YOUR SUPERHERO USE HIS SUPERPOWERS TO RETURN BULLYTOR TO PRISON?

BULLYTOR

- HAS THE ABILITY TO THROW INSULT BALLS (SILVER BALLS FILLED WITH MEAN INSULTS)
- CAN FLY
- LIKES TO FIGHT (KICK, SHOVE, HIT)
- CAN MAKE PEOPLE CRY
- TELLS MEAN "YO MAMA" JOKES
- CAN PICK OUT A VICTIM'S PERSONAL WEAKNESS IN 2 SECONDS

Reproducible Lesson 5

HOW TO MAKE A SUPERHERO FLIP BOOK

What is a flip book?
A flip book is a book that has pictures that appear to move when the pages are turned quickly.

You will need:
Paper
Scissors
Stapler
Ruler
Your Brain

Step 1: Cut several pieces of paper to size and staple them together on one end.

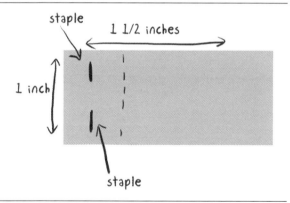

Step 2: Start your drawing on the last page of the flip book.

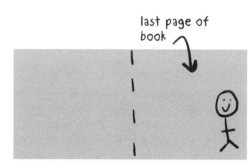

Reproducible Lesson 5

Step 3: To make the image look like it is moving, draw the same image, but make it move a little on each page.

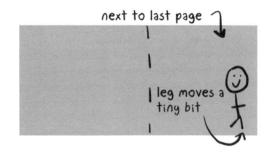

Step 4: Continue Step 3 until you reach the next to last page.

Step 5: Give the book a title and add some cover art.

Step 6: Flip the pages backward and forwards to see your drawings move!

For more fun, color your drawings!

HOW TO MAKE A COMIC STRIP

Step 1: Select a comic book page template, or draw your own panels with squares, rectangles, or other cool shapes.

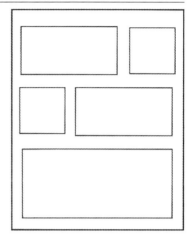

Step 2: Sketch your comic in the panels with a pencil.

Step 3: When you are happy with your panels, go over the pencil lines with a black pen.

Step 4: Color in your comic using colored pencils.

Step 5: Take the cover of the comic (made in Lesson 4) and cut another piece of construction paper the same size (this will be the back cover).

Step 6: Staple the pages of the comic between the front and back covers.

Step 7: Enjoy!

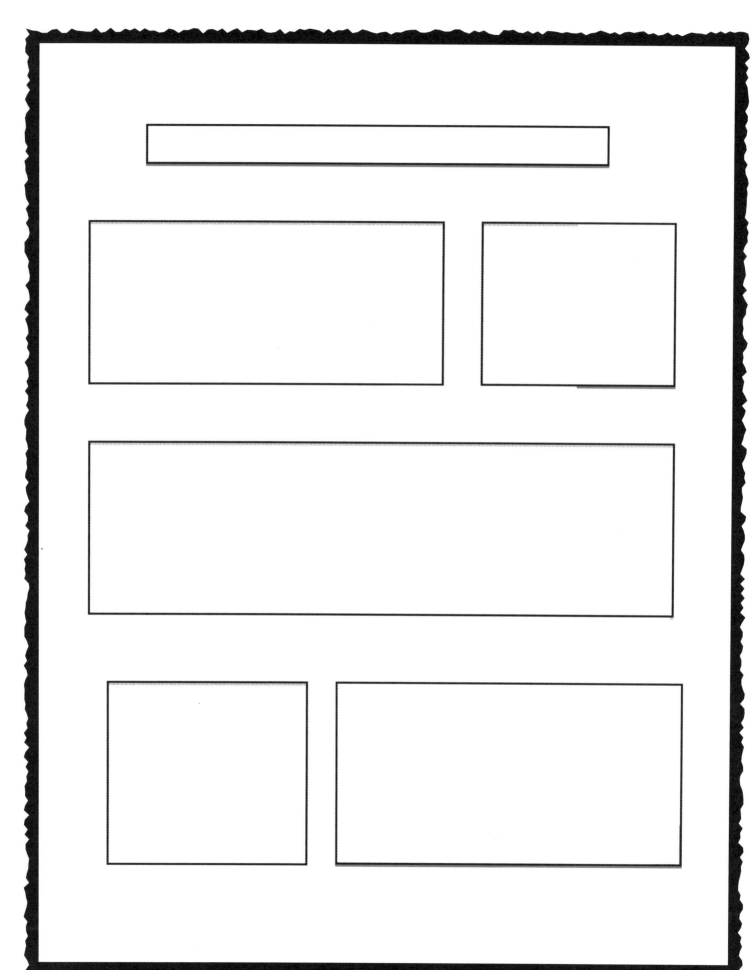

Reproducible Lesson 5

SUPER COUNSELOR EXTENSION ACTIVITIES FOR LESSON 5!

EXTENSION ACTIVITY #1: QUICK QUOTE

Materials:

- Copies of the Quote Worksheet
- Pens or pencils

Quote:

"I'm a hero with coward's legs." – S. Milligan

QUICK QUOTE

"I'm a hero with coward's legs." – S. Milligan

- Write this quote in your own words. You can ask group members for help!

_____
_____
_____
_____
_____

- Can a hero be brave and scared at the same time?

_____
_____
_____
_____
_____

- Tell about a time when you were scared and brave at the same time.

_____
_____
_____
_____
_____
_____

EXTENSION ACTIVITY #2: BULLY MAD LIB

Materials:

- Copies of the Bully Mad Lib
- Pens or pencils

BULLY MAD LIB!

(FILL IN THE BLANKS WITH YOUR OWN FUNNY WORDS!)

Once upon a time there was a very _____ superhero who lived on the
                                      (adjective)

planet _____ . His name was _____ . His superpowers
       (silly planet name)   (Superhero name)

included the ability to _____ , to _____ , and to _____ .
                        (verb) (verb)   (verb)

One day, _____ , noticed that a bully was _____ ing
         (Superhero name)   (action verb)

two helpless _____ s at the _____ . _____
             (noun)   (place)   (Superhero name)

sprang into action! He _____ over to the bully and used his
                       (action verb)

special super _____ to turn the bully into a _____ !
              (noun)   (noun)

Then he used his _____ to send the bully to _____ ,
                 (noun)   (place)

where he could never bully again!   Everyone cheered and clapped for

_____ , who bowed to the crowed and then _____
(Superhero name)   (action verb)

into the _____ .
         (place)

THE END

Reproducible Lesson 5

COMIC BOOK ROLE PLAY

Role-play is a great way to help teach social skills! It allows group members to try new personas and use new skill sets in a safe and fun environment.

Materials:

- Magic Counselor Box
- Group member's comic books
- Magic Role Play Suitcase – a big suitcase filled with any and all kinds of dress up clothes and accessories. Hats, ties, swords, umbrellas, suit jackets, wedding dresses, wigs, etc. Take a trip to the local thrift store – who knows what you might find!

Activity:

1. Each member chooses a scene from their comic where their superhero is using real life skills to deal with Bullytor (ex. ignoring, walking away, using humor, etc.).
2. Members can select group members to help with the reenactment of the comic.
3. Members can use items from the Magic Role Play Suitcase to help plan their scene.
4. The scene is acted out for the group.
5. After the scene, the counselor can use these follow-up questions:
   - What was the main problem in the scene?
   - How did the superhero defeat Bullytor?
   - How could you use this/these skills in real life?
   - How could the superhero help other targets with his skills?
   - What was it like to be Bullytor?
   - What was it like to be the superhero?
   - What was it like to be the target?

Lesson 6:
The Way of the Samurai

Objectives:

- Boys will examine the Way of the Samurai
- Boys will discuss the Warrior Virtues
- Boys will create their own samurai mask

Materials:

- Magic Counselor Box
- Poster of Group Oath and Hand Signs for the wall

Copies:

- Japanese Symbols sheet
- Samurai Virtues worksheet
- SSBS

Opening

- Group members sit in a circle. Try to have members sit by members they do not know well.
- Recite Group Oath with secret hand signs.

1. Give out the **Samurai Virtues** handout. Pick members to read aloud the character words and definitions one at a time. Give members time to write responses to each word question. Ask members to share what they have written.

2. Group leader reads the **Way of the Warrior**.

3. Listening Comprehension Questions:

- Who were the samurai?
- What is a life path?
- Explain the Way of the Warrior
- What virtue do you believe is most important? Share your reasons.
- The samurai were not only warriors, but also celebrated artists and musicians. How does that fit into your personal view of masculinity?
- The samurai thought it was better not to fight to solve problems. What do you think of this?

Activity: Samurai Mask

Samurai Mask

The samurai wore elaborate masks when they went into battle. The warriors deliberately made the masks as frightening as possible, so that they would be a terrifying sight to their enemy. The masks were embellished with Japanese symbols and colors, which represented the particular virtues of the wearer.

a. Hand out the Japanese Symbols worksheet.

b. Ask members to select 2 symbols to decorate each side of their samurai mask.

c. Use the directions in the "Making a Samurai Mask" section.

1. Have members place worksheets in their BCBH.
2. Have members color in Lesson 4 on the pie chart in their handbook.

Follow-up

- Ask the boys the following questions:
    - Tell us about your mask. Tell us why you picked those colors and symbols.
    - What part of the mask design is most important to you?
    - Explain what you like best about another group member's mask.

Evaluation

- Observe the attention level of the boys as they discuss the Way of the Warrior.

- Note the Japanese symbols and colors members chose to put on their mask. Do these symbols accurately represent the member? Why or why not?

- If a member seems reluctant to participate, meet with them privately to discuss their problems or concerns.

Individual Counseling

Time: 50 minutes

1. Client and counselor read the Way of the Warrior together (each read the alternating paragraph)

2. The following questions can be used to stimulate discussion:

    - Who were the samurai?
    - What is a life path?
    - Explain the Way of the Warrior
    - What virtue do you believe is most important? Share your reasons.
    - The samurai were not only warriors, but also celebrated artists and musicians. How does that fit into your personal view of masculinity?
    - The samurai thought it was better not to fight to solve problems. What do you think of this?

3. Use the directions in the "Making a Samurai Mask" section.

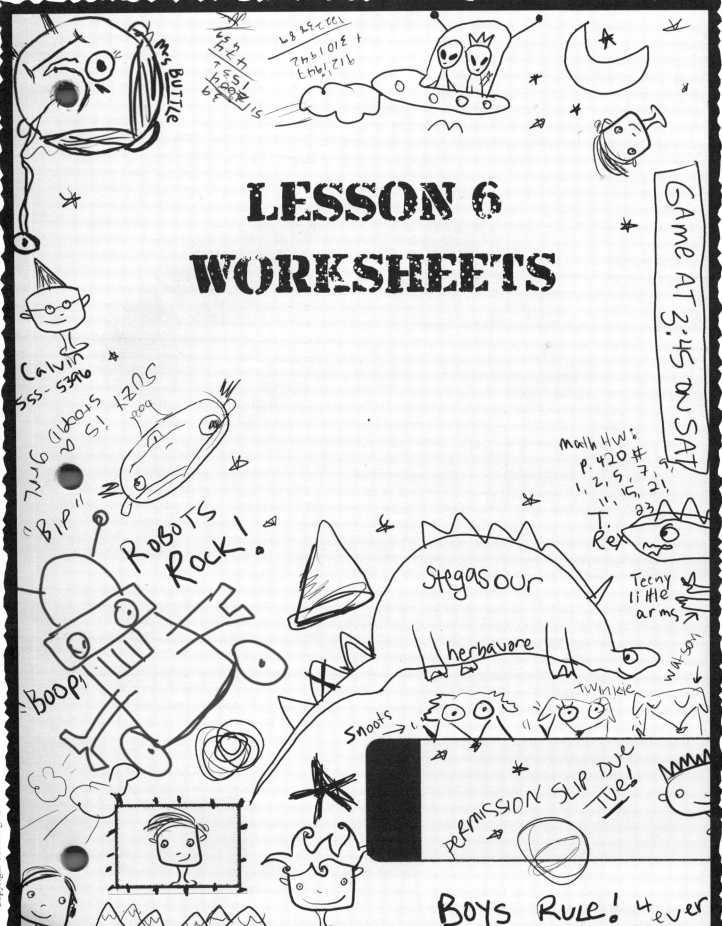

The Samurai Virtues

☯ Rectitude - telling the truth

Write about a time when you told the truth, even when it was hard.

_____
_____
_____

☯ Benevolence - charitable kindness

How can you show benevolence at home and at school?

_____
_____
_____

☯ Wisdom - gaining knowledge and personal experience

What words of wisdom can you give a 1st or 2nd grader about life? How does wisdom change you?

_____
_____
_____

☯ Courage - ability to do things one finds frightening

Tell about a time when you showed great courage.

_____
_____
_____
_____

Reproducible Lesson 6

The Way of the Warrior

The Samurai were a noble group of courageous warriors. They lived in Japan almost 700 years ago. Legend holds that these warriors were the most skillful swordsmen, martial artists, and military leaders in the history of world.

The Samurai were not just soldiers who could use a sword. This brotherhood of highly intelligent men followed a path of life known as Bushido, or the Way of The Warrior.

The Way of the Warrior is a way of living one's life according to the following tenets:

- **Rectitude** – telling the truth
- **Courage** – the ability to do things one finds frightening
- **Benevolence** – showing charitable kindness
- **Respect** – acting courteously towards yourself and others
- **Honesty** – speaking the truth
- **Honor** – having a good reputation, keeping one's word
- **Loyalty** – to be faithful to one's family, friends, and personal beliefs

The goal of the samurai was to protect the people and fight for what is right. Although they could kill a man instantly with their bare hands, the samurai thought it was nobler to settle differences without ever resorting to physical violence.

Most samurai were not only skilled in combat, but they were accomplished artists and musicians as well. The samurai were educated men who believed that one man's positive actions could change the world.

Japanese Symbols and Their Meanings

Instead of writing in words, the Japanese draw little pictures, or Kanji, to represent the object. They weave Kanji along with letters from the Japanese alphabet to make sentences. Japanese writing is read from top to bottom and from right to left!

| **The Way of the Warrior** | **Courage** | **Honesty** |

| **Respect** | **Honor** | **Loyalty** |

Reproducible Lesson 6

知恵	努力	友情
Wisdom	**Effort**	**Friendship**
平和	仁	礼
Peace	**Compassion**	**Courtesy**
運命	調和	家族
Destiny	**Harmony**	**Family**

Make an Origami Fox!

Origami is the ancient art of Japanese paper folding.

What You Will Need:
Square piece of thin paper
Your Brain

Step 1: Fold the square paper in half. Make sure the crease is even and tight.

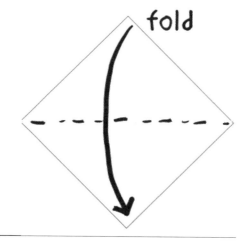
fold

Step 2: Fold both of the points down, keeping the points together.

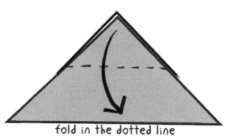
fold in the dotted line

Step 3: Fold both sides in to the center to make the fox's ears.

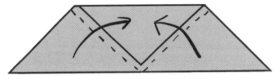

Fold in the dotted line

Step 4: Turn the paper over.

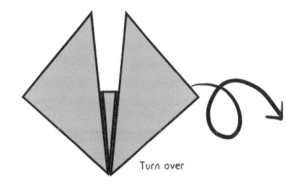

Turn over

Step 5: Draw in the fox's eyes and nose.

Draw in the fox's face

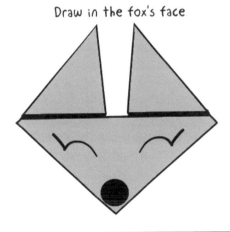

Step 6: Enjoy!

How to Make a Samurai Mask

Step 1: Enlarge the Samurai Mask template and draw on poster board.

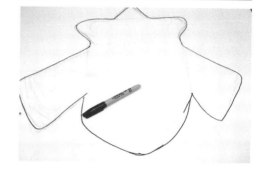

Step 2: Cut out the mask.

Step 3: Take a piece of construction paper (in desired symbolic color(s). Using the mask as a guide, cut 2 side flaps out of the construction paper.

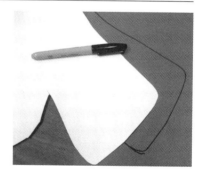

Step 4: Glue one construction paper side flap to the mask.

Reproducible Lesson 6

Step 5: Glue the other construction paper side flap to the masks.

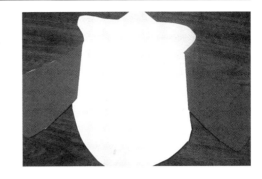

Step 6: Using the mask as a guide, cut out a piece of construction paper to cover the "crown" of the mask.

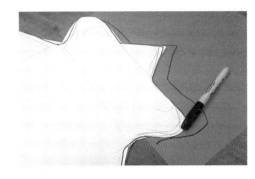

Step 7: Cut out the crown.

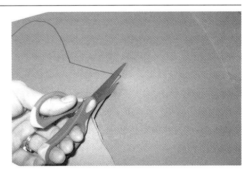

Step 8: Glue crown to top of mask.

Step 9: Sketch eyes onto masks.

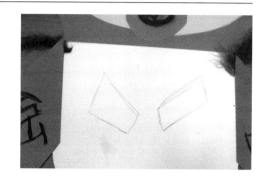

Step 10a: To cut out eyes, first poke a hole in one of the corners.

Step 10b: Stick one end of scissors into the hole and cut out the eye.

Step 11: Use Japanese symbols, colors, and magic embellishments to decorate the mask.

Step 12: Enjoy!

Reproducible Lesson 6

Samurai Mask Template

SUPER COUNSELOR EXTENSION ACTIVITIES FOR LESSON 6!

EXTENSION ACTIVITY #1: QUICK QUOTE

Materials:

- Copies of the Quote Worksheet
- Pens or pencils

Quote:

"Master the divine teachings of the Art of Peace and no enemy will dare to challenge you." - Ueshiba

QUICK QUOTE

"Master the divine teachings of the Art of Peace and no enemy will dare to challenge you." - Ueshiba

- Write this quote in your own words. You can ask group members for help!

_____
_____
_____
_____

- What is the "Art of Peace"?

_____
_____
_____

- Why is it better to solve conflicts with words rather than physical violence?

_____
_____
_____

- Tell about a time when you solved conflicts with words.

_____
_____
_____
_____

EXTENSION ACTIVITY #2: THE WAY OF THE WARRIOR PLEDGE

Materials:

- Magic Counselor Box
- Copies of The Way of the Warrior Pledge

Activity:

1. Discuss with members the meaning of a pledge.

    - What is a pledge? (pledge – a promise to do something)
    - The samurai, like the Knights of the Round Table, made a pledge to the people of their lands. How are their pledges alike?
    - Can you make a pledge to yourself?

2. Read the Way of the Warrior Pledge.

    - If you took this pledge, what changes would you have to make in your life?
    - Is it easier to make a pledge with a group of friends? How could your friends help you stick to your pledge?

3. Encourage members to take the pledge for one week. At the end of the week, use the Way of the Warrior Pledge Follow Up.

The Way of the Warrior Pledge

I pledge to live the Way of the Warrior for one week. I will:

- Protect and stand up for anyone I see getting teased or bullied

- Respect the differences in others

- Help those in need — without being asked

- Spend at least 20 minutes each day doing physical activity (running, playing sports, swimming).

- Complete all my class work and turn in all homework assignments

- Follow my parents' or teachers' directions — the first time they ask

_____   _____
Signed   Date

Way of the Warrior Pledge Follow-up:

1. What was it like to keep a pledge for a week? Was it hard or easy? What made it hard? What made it easy?

2. What changes did you have to make in your behavior?

3. What was the most difficult part of the pledge for you?

4. Did you help a friend keep his pledge? Did a friend help you keep your pledge?

5. Will you continue to follow the pledge in the future?

EXTRA FUN FOR DARING COUNSELORS:

Koinobori: Flying Fish

Every year the Japanese celebrate Children's Day, a day dedicated to celebrating the spirit of children. The symbol of Children's Day is the koinobori, or "flying fish." The koi, or carp fish, is a strong fish with the amazing ability to swim up waterfalls! In Japan, the koi is a symbol of courage and strength.

On Children's Day, Japanese families fly koinobori from their homes to honor and encourage these characteristics in their sons. Koinobori are brightly painted and range in size from a few feet to several yards long.

Materials:

- Magic Counselor Box
- Large rolls of multicolor paper

How to Make a Koinobori

Step 1: Cut a piece of colored roll paper about 3 feet wide by 4 feet high.

Step 2: Cut the large paper in half.

Step 3: Place one piece of the paper on top of the other.

Step 4: Sketch the fish body onto the top paper.

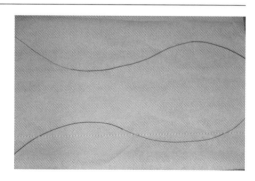

Reproducible Lesson 6

Step 5: With the 2 pieces together, cut out the fish shape.

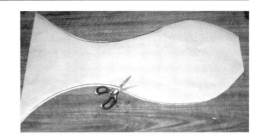

Step 6: Using construction paper, cut out and glue on eyes, fins, and scales

Step 7: Staple the 2 pieces of the fish together around the edges.

Step 8: Cut wavy streamers out of construction paper.

Step 9: Attach streamers to the bottom of the fish with the stapler.

Step 10: Cut out a 1-inch strip wide piece of poster board approximately 8 inches long.

Step 11: Staple the poster board strip into a circle.

Step 12: Fit the poster board circle into the fish's mouth.

Step 13: Staple the cardboard circle to the inside of the fish's mouth. This makes the mouth open wide.

Step 14: Punch a hole on each side of the fish's mouth (punch through the paper and the cardboard).

Step 15: String yarn through the 2 holes and tie together.

Step 16:

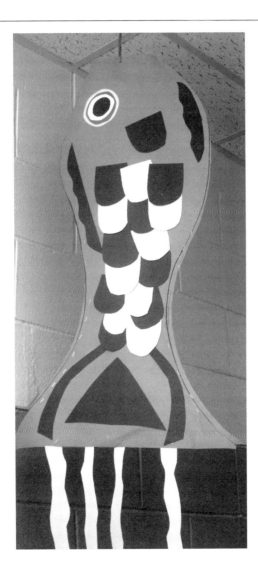 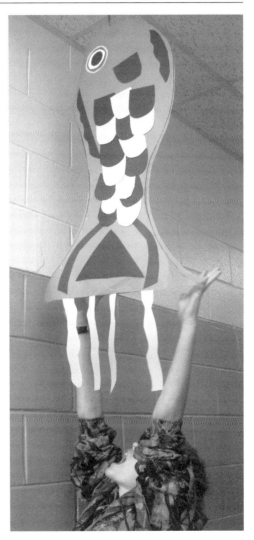

Hang from a high place. Enjoy!

Lesson 7:
The Magic Circle

Objectives:

- Boys will learn about the Magic Circle
- Boys will discuss the Magician's Code
- Boys will learn and present their own magic tricks

Materials:

- Magic Counselor Box
- Decks of cards
- Ash (can be obtained from a fireplace, an ashtray, or by burning matches in a bowl and then smashing the burnt wood into powder)
- Coke cans
- Napkins, paper towels
- Coins

Copies:

- Magic Circle worksheets
- Magician's Code worksheets
- 3 magic tricks (one for each member)

You will want to learn how to do the magic tricks before the lesson. This way, you can provide a visual demonstration to the group!

Opening

- Group members sit in a circle. Try to have members sit by members they do not know well.

- Recite Group Oath with secret hand signs.

1. Group leader reads the The Magic Circle

2. Listening Comprehension Questions:

    - Why did the magicians form The Magic Circle?
    - Lots of groups have mottos. What is a motto? How does a motto guide group members? Tell the group about any mottos you know about.
    - What does the Magician's Motto mean? Why is it important to group members?
    - How does the Magician's Code protect magicians?

3. The Magician's Code

    Hand out The Magician's Code worksheet. Use the following script as a guide for discussion.

    Each part of the Magician's Code is related to a character trait. Let's talk about these traits and what they mean:

    Have members read each part of the Magician's code. Discuss the meaning of the character trait:

    - **Responsibility** – be accountable for your choices, do what you are supposed to do, be self-disciplined
    - **Respect** – following the Golden Rule, be considerate of others
    - **Fairness** – Don't take advantage of others
    - **Trustworthiness** – Don't deceive, cheat, or steal
    - **Caring** – be kind and compassionate

Activity: Making Magic!

1. Group leader demonstrates The Ash Trick, Coke Can Through Table, and The Reversed Card.

2. Group leader hands out the instructions for each trick, along with the supplies (decks of cards, ash, etc.)

3. Members practice each trick, using each other as audience members.

1. Have members place worksheets in their BCBH.
2. Have members color in Lesson 7 on the pie chart in their handbook.

Follow-up

- Ask the boys the following questions:
    - Why do you think magicians should not perform a trick more than once in front of the same audience?
    - Are magic tricks a kind of secret? Explain.
    - Why do you think the magicians formed a magic club?

Evaluation

- Observe the attention level of the boys as they discuss the The Magician's Code.

- Personally encourage members who seem particularly interested in magic to check out books from the library on magic, magical history, and magician biographies. Or check out youthlightbooks.com for ones that can be purchased.

- If a member seems reluctant to participate, meet with them privately to discuss their problems or concerns.

Individual Counseling

Time: 50 minutes

1. Client and counselor read The Magician's Code together (each read the alternating paragraph)

2. Using The Magician's Code worksheet, go through each character trait and discuss.

3. Use the directions in the Activity section.

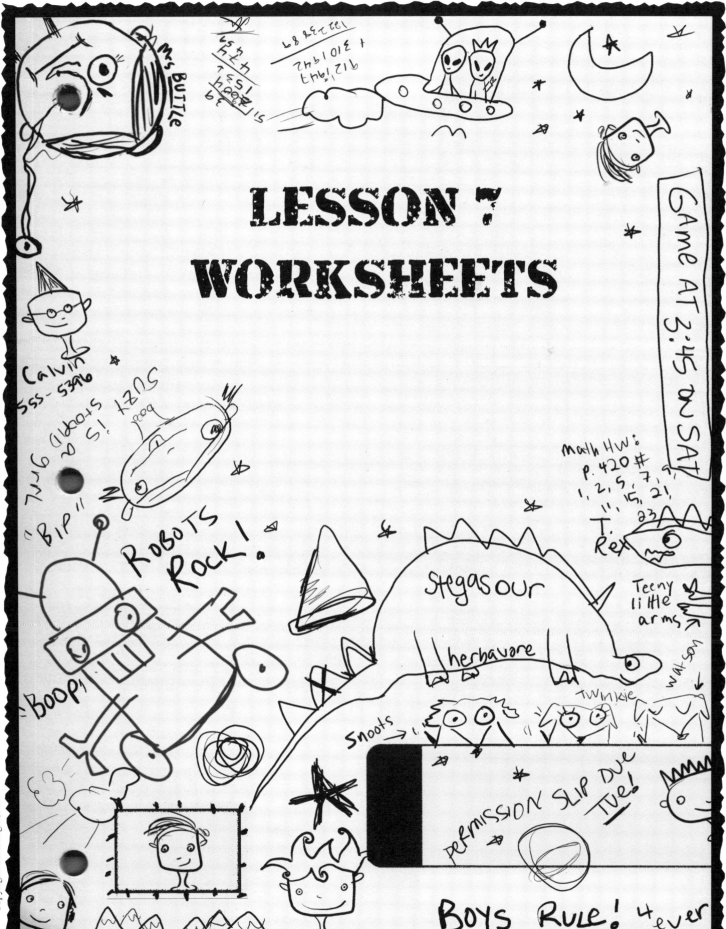

The Magic Circle

In 1905, a group of magicians in London, England, decided to form a magic club. The purpose of the club would be to work together as a group to learn more about magic tricks and illusions, to help each other become better performers, and to protect the secrets of magic from non-magicians.

The members of the Magic Circle pledged to live by the Magician's Motto and Code. The Magician's Motto, written in Latin, reads *"indocilis privata loqui"* which means "not apt to disclose secrets." Simply stated, the Magician's Code says:

1. I will not expose any magic secrets in public.

2. If someone else is doing a magic trick, and I know how it works, I will not tell the audience how it works.

3. I will not steal a trick that someone else has created and say that it is mine.

4. I will not claim to have supernatural powers.

5. If I use animals in my magic tricks, I will not harm them.

6. I will never do a trick twice in front of the same audience.

7. I will never perform a trick in front of an audience unless I can perform it perfectly each time.

In order for new members to join the club, they must first be able to perfectly perform several magic tricks. They will then meet with the members of the Circle to show their skills. If the Circle is impressed with their skills, they will allow the individual to join the club. The young member is expected to continue to learn new tricks and pass examinations to continue membership in the club.

The Magician's Code

Responsibility: I will not expose any magic secrets in public.

Responsibility -
_____
_____
_____

Respect: If someone else is doing a magic trick, and I know how it works, I will not tell the audience how it works.

Respect -
_____
_____
_____

Fairness: I will not steal a trick that someone else has created and say that it is mine.

Fairness-
_____
_____
_____

Trustworthiness: I will not claim to have supernatural powers.

Trustworthiness-
_____
_____
_____

Caring: If I use animals in my magic tricks, I will not harm them.

Caring-
_____
_____
_____

The Ash Trick

The Ash Trick is a classic trick that always astounds the audience!

The Effect:
The magician takes some ash and rubs it into the spectators clenched fist until they disappear. He then says some magic words and asks the spectator to open their fist to reveal that the ash has penetrated onto their palm!

Preparation:
Secretly put some ash on your middle fingers.

Step 1: Tell the spectator to stand in front of you and hold their hands out towards you, palms down.

Tell them to come a little closer and physically take their hands to gently pull the person a little closer.

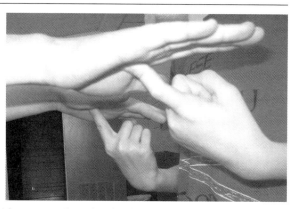

At the same time touch their palm lightly with the ash on your middle finger.

Reproducible Lesson 7

Step 2: Ask them to close their fists, then rub some ash on their fist and rub in until it disappears.

Step 3: Say some magic words and do some make magical hand waves.

Then, ask them to open their hands to see that the ash seems to have penetrated their fist!

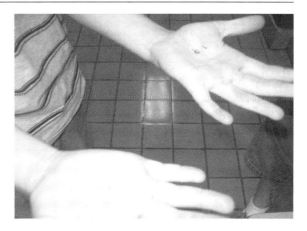

Magician's Tip: Never, never do the same trick twice! The audience will catch on the second time!

Soda Can Through Table

The Effect
You magically make a soda can pass through a table!

Preparation:
You will need a coin, an empty or closed coke can, and some paper napkins or paper towels.

Step 1: Place the coin on the table. Tell the audience that you are going to make the coin pass through the table.

Step 2: Cover the coke can with the napkins. Make sure that the whole can is covered.

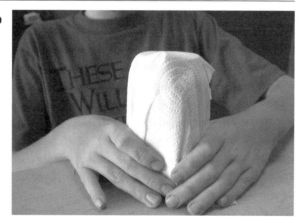

Step 3: Place the coke can over the coin.

Step 4: Have an audience member count to three.

Step 5: Say a magic word and lift up the coke can with the napkins. (the coin will still be there)

Step 6: Hold the coke can over your lap while saying, "Oh, it didn't work..."

Step 7: While you keep your eyes on the can, quietly drop the soda can from the napkin, while holding the napkin's form. (The can should land on your lap.)

Step 8: Move the napkin to the middle of the table, still holding the shape of the can.

Step 9: Push the top of the napkin down to the table so that it looks like the can melted through the table.

Step 10: Pull the shaker out from under the table. Say "Oh yeah, I forgot! This trick makes the soda can go through the table!"

The Reversed Card

The Effect:
An audience member selects a card and places it back into the deck. After placing the deck behind your back and bringing it out again, the selected card is shown to have reversed itself in the **deck!**

Preparation:

You will need a deck of cards. Prepare the deck by reversing the bottom card so it faces the opposite way. **Never let the audience see that the bottom card is reversed!**

You have secretly reversed the top card so the deck looks as if it's face-down when it's really face-up.

When the audience member puts his card back into the deck, it is reversed and facing the other way.

Step 1: Take out the deck and spread the cards so the audience member may choose one.

Be careful that you don't show the bottom card that is reversed and facing the other way.

Reproducible Lesson 7

Step 2: You Say:

"Sir, if you would please show your card to the audience, so that they may memorize it."

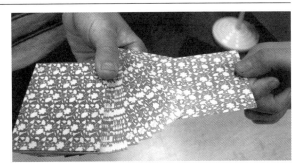

While the audience member is showing his card, you turn the deck over so the reversed card is on top. As long as you hold the deck together without spreading the cards, it will look as if the deck is face down.

Step 3: Hold the deck tightly, so it won't spread open. Take the card from the audience member (don't look at the face of the card!) and slide it into the deck.

Step 4: Put the deck behind your back and secretly turn over the top card.

The selected card is now the only one in the deck that is facing the other way.

Step 5: Bring out the deck with all the cards facing up. Spread the deck out on a table. The selected card will be face down.

Slowly turn over the selected card to reveal it as the chosen card!

Reproducible Lesson 7

Make a Message in Invisible Ink!

What You Will Need:
Lemon Juice
A toothpick or Q-tip
A piece of paper
Your Brain

Step 1: Pour lemon juice into a bowl. Dip the toothpick tip into the lemon juice.

Step 2: Write your note on the paper with the toothpick. Load the toothpick with more juice for each letter.

Step 3: Allow the paper to dry. As the paper dries, your message will disappear.

Step 4: To reveal the secret message, hold the paper a few inches from a light bulb. As the paper gets warm, the message will begin to appear!

SUPER COUNSELOR EXTENSION ACTIVITIES FOR LESSON 7!

EXTENSION ACTIVITY #1: QUICK QUOTE

Materials:

- Copies of the Quote Worksheet
- Pens or pencils

Quote:

"Magic is believing in yourself, if you can do that, anything can happen." – Goethe

QUICK QUOTE

"Magic is believing in yourself, if you can do that, anything can happen." – Goethe

- Write this quote in your own words. You can ask group members for help!

    _____
    _____
    _____
    _____

- Is it hard to believe in yourself all the time?

    _____
    _____
    _____
    _____

- Name 3 people who believe in you. Explain how they support you.

    _____
    _____
    _____
    _____
    _____

- List 3 things you can tell yourself when you are having a hard time believing in your abilities.

    _____
    _____
    _____
    _____
    _____

Reproducible Lesson 7

EXTENSION ACTIVITY #2: LEARNING YOUR OWN TRICK

This activity can be done in a group session or you can assign this activity for homework.

Materials:

- Access to magic trick books or the internet
- Supplies for new tricks (can be purchased through youthlightbooks.com)

Activity:

1. Have members research a magic trick that interests them.
2. Assist members in collecting necessary objects required for the trick.
3. Encourage members to practice the trick until they are able to perform it flawlessly for the group.
4. Hold a mini magic circle seminar where group members teach each other their tricks.

Extra Fun for Daring Counselors:

Planning and Performing a Magic Show

If you feel that your group is ready, help them plan a simple magic show. Each member can perform one or two tricks.

Potential audiences include:

- K-3 classes
- Parents
- Teachers
- Nursing homes

Lesson 8:
INITIATION

Objectives:

- Boys will discuss the meaning of a rite of passage
- Boys will be initiated into the Boy Code Brotherhood
- Boys will discuss their experience in the group

Materials:

- Magic Counselor Box
- Individualized Certificates
- Candle for each group member (any inexpensive candles are fine, just make sure that they have a holder for the wax)
- 2 Candles for the counselor
- Long tip lighter candle
- 8 Initiation Envelopes
- Camera (if possible to take a group shot for the BC Book)
- Snack – cookies or cake, and a drink

Copies:

- Initiation Secrets 1-8
- My Initiation Affirmation
- Boy Code Certificates
- Boy Code Photo Page (optional)

Pre-Group Prep:

- If possible, darken the room for a more mysterious, momentus effect

- Copy the INITIATION SECRETS sheets and seal each in one envelope. Write the number of the secret on the front of the envelope.

- Complete the INITIATION AFFIRMATION worksheet for each member

Opening

- Group members sit in a circle.

- Recite Group Oath with secret hand signs.

Initiation Ceremony

Counselor:

A rite of passage is when we celebrate a life transition. We honor the old part of our life and look forward to a new way of living. Some examples of rites of passage include birthdays, weddings, and death. Today we will be celebrating a rite of passage for you! You will be initiated into the Boy Code Brotherhood. Because you have worked together through the Seven Lessons, you will learn secrets only you and your fellow group members will know.

1. Give each member a small candle and 1 sealed initiation envelope. Give envelope #1 to the member on your right side (Boy #1), envelope #2 to the next member (Boy #2) until each member has 1 envelope. If there are less than 8 group members, the counselor keeps the remaining envelopes.

2. Tell the members to put the envelope in front of them and place their candle on top of the envelope.

3. Counselor places 2 candles in front of her/him on the table. (There are 8 secrets. If you have less than 8 group members, you will add an extra candle to your set. For instance, if you only had 6 group members, you would put 4 candles in front of yourself (2 for you and 2 for the other 2 secrets, which you will read)

4. Using the long candle lighter, counselor lights first candle

Counselor:

Over the past weeks I have seen a positive change in each of you. You have learned about different types of masculinity and explored what it means to become a man.

Turn to the boy on your right side (Boy #1). Read him the Individual Affirmation you have written for him.

Counselor:

(asks Boy #1) **"Have you completed all the lessons and colored the marks in your book?"**

Boy # 1: Yes.

Counselor:

(asks Boy #1) **Do your brothers agree this to be so?** (counselor looks at group members) **If any you can say with truth that this brother has completed all his lessons for initiation say "Yea" now.** (counselor may need to encourage members to say "yea."

Group Members: "Yea"

Counselor:

(to Boy #1) **"Then I find you worthy to open the seal on the first secret and read it aloud to your brothers."**

(counselor gives lighter to Boy #1)

Boy #1 (opens his envelope and reads the paragraph aloud):

*"I light this candle to honor my brothers and to reveal the first secret of our group **(light your candle)**. Our Latin motto Amicitia, fortitudo et pertinacia, means friendship, courage, and determination. We have become friends over the last eight weeks. When we tried new experiences and shared our personal thoughts and feelings, we proved that we are courageous. We have shown determination in the fact that we completed all our lessons and stand here today, together, as a true brotherhood."*

Turn to the next boy on your right side (Boy #2). Read him the Individual Affirmation you have written for him.

Counselor:

(asks Boy #2) **"Have you completed all the lessons and colored the marks in your book?"**

Boy # 2: Yes.

Counselor:

(asks Boy #2) **Do your brothers agree this to be so?** (counselor looks at group members) **If any you can say with truth that this brother has completed all his lessons for initiation say "Yea" now.** (counselor may need to encourage members to say "yea."

Group Members: "Yea"

Counselor:

(to Boy #2) **"Then I find you worthy to open the seal on the second secret and read it aloud to your brothers."**

Boy #2 (opens his envelope and reads the paragraph aloud):

*"I light this candle to honor my brothers and to reveal the second secret of our group **(light your candle)**. This is the secret meaning of the lion on our crest. The lion has a sun for a mane. The lion stands for leadership, strength, courage, honor, and loyalty. The sun represents knowledge and warmth. Together they are a shining symbol of what a real man can be."*

Turn to the next boy on your right side (Boy #3). Read him the Individual Affirmation you have written for him.

Counselor:

(asks Boy #3) **"Have you completed all the lessons and colored the marks in your book?"**

Boy # 3: Yes.

Counselor: (asks Boy #3) **Do your brothers agree this to be so?** (counselor looks at group members) **If any you can say with truth that this brother has completed all his lessons for initiation say "Yea" now.** (counselor may need to encourage members to say "yea."

Group Members: "Yea"

Counselor:

(to Boy #3) **"Then I find you worthy to open the seal on the third secret and read it aloud to your brothers."**

Boy #3 (opens his envelope and reads the paragraph aloud):

*"I light this candle to honor my brothers and to reveal the third secret of our group **(light your candle)**. The lines on the sides of the crest represent wings. When we follow our hearts and are true to ourselves, we can soar to great heights."*

Turn to the next boy on your right side (Boy #4). Read him the Individual Affirmation you have written for him.

Counselor:

(asks Boy #4) **Do your brothers agree this to be so?** (counselor looks at group members) **If any you can say with truth that this brother has completed all his lessons for initiation say "Yea" now.** (counselor may need to encourage members to say "yea."

Group Members: "Yea"

Counselor:

(to Boy #4) **"Then I find you worthy to open the seal on the fourth secret and read it aloud to your brothers."**

Boy #4 (opens his envelope and reads the paragraph aloud):

*"I light this candle to honor my brothers and to reveal the fourth secret of our group **(light your candle)**. This is the secret meaning of the candle on our crest. The candle stands for a light in the darkness. Each of us is a tiny light in the darkness. Our lights burn brighter for every good deed we do to help our brothers and mankind. The candle reminds us to always strive to be a light in all places."*

Turn to the next boy on your right side (Boy #5). Read him the Individual Affirmation you have written for him.

Counselor:

(asks Boy #5) **Do your brothers agree this to be so?** (counselor looks at group members) **If any you can say with truth that this brother has completed all his** lessons for initiation say "Yea" now. (counselor may need to encourage members to say "yea."

Group Members: "Yea"

Counselor:

(to Boy #5) **"Then I find you worthy to open the seal on the fifth secret and read it aloud to your brothers."**

Boy #5 (opens his envelope and reads the paragraph aloud):

*"I light this candle to honor my brothers and to reveal the fifth secret of our group **(light your candle)**. This is the secret meaning of the ship on our crest. The ship is heading east. East represents new experiences and new horizons. The ship is a symbol of joy, happiness, and adventure. Thus, this part of the crest reminds us that life is waiting to be lived and explored."*

Turn to the next boy on your right side (Boy #6). Read him the Individual Affirmation you have written for him.

Counselor:

(asks Boy #6) **Do your brothers agree this to be so? (counselor looks at group members) If any you can say with truth that this brother has completed all his lessons for initiation say "Yea" now.** (counselor may need to encourage members to say "yea."

Group Members: "Yea"

Counselor:

(to Boy #6) **"Then I find you worthy to open the seal on the sixth secret and read it aloud to your brothers."**

Boy #6 (opens his envelope and reads the paragraph aloud):

*"I light this candle to honor my brothers and to reveal the sixth secret of our group **(light your candle)**. This is the secret meaning of the heart on our crest. It reminds us to follow our hearts. We should listen to our feelings and make choices based on what we believe is right for us. Brothers, I bid you remember - know thyself."*

Turn to the next boy on your right side (Boy #7). Read him the Individual Affirmation you have written for him.

Counselor:

(asks Boy #7) **Do your brothers agree this to be so?** (counselor looks at group members) **If any you can say with truth that this brother has completed all his lessons for initiation say "Yea" now.** (counselor may need to encourage members to say "yea."

Group Members: "Yea"

Counselor:

(to Boy #7) **"Then I find you worthy to open the seal on the seventh secret and read it aloud to your brothers."**

Boy #7 (opens his envelope and reads the paragraph aloud):

*"I light this candle to honor my brothers and to reveal the seventh secret of our group **(light your candle)**. On the bottom left swirl of the crest lies a line and three dots. This is the Japanese symbol for mind, heart, and spirit. We now know that no one can be a real man unless they honor each of these areas in their life."*

Turn to the next boy on your right side (Boy #8). Read him the Individual Affirmation you have written for him.

Counselor:

(asks Boy #8) **Do your brothers agree this to be so?** (counselor looks at group members) **If any you can say with truth that this brother has completed all his lessons for initiation say "Yea" now.** (counselor may need to encourage members to say "yea."

Group Members: "Yea"

Counselor:

(to Boy #8) **"Then I find you worthy to open the seal on the seventh secret and read it aloud to your brothers."**

Boy #8 (opens his envelope and reads the paragraph aloud):

*"I light this candle to honor my brothers and to reveal the eighth and final secret of our group **(light your candle)**. On the bottom right hand side of our crest is a turning spiral. When we do a good deed, it sets a spiral of change in motion. Your good deed prompts someone else to do a good deed,*

and so on until our one action creates a spiral of good for all those around us. Brothers, I encourage you to be the kind of person who starts many, many, spirals in life."

(once all the secrets have been read, the counselor lights the 2nd candle)

Congratulations. Now you know all the secrets of our group. You have worked hard, you have learned a great deal about your brothers, and most importantly, you have learned about yourself. I am so proud of you, and I admire you for your friendship, your courage, and your determination. I am so proud of each of you, and I know that you have the power to change the world!

Now……let's eat!

Follow-up

While the group is snacking, ask the boys the following questions:

- What was it like to be initiated?
- What was your favorite part of the initiation?
- What does it mean to be initiated?
- How do you feel about the crest now that you know all the secrets it holds?
- What are 2 things you learned about yourself during the group?
- Was it hard to get to know the other group members?
- What is something you learned about another member that surprised you?
- What will you remember most about the group?

Evaluation

- Observe the attention level of the boys as they proceed through the initiation session.
- Are any members upset by the termination of the group? How can you help them?
- If a member seems reluctant to participate, meet with them privately to discuss their problems or concerns.

Individual Counseling

Time: 50 minutes

In an individual session, the counselor and client can light a candle. Using a copy of the crest, the counselor and client can discuss the meaning of each part of the crest, and how the client can use these ideals in his own life. Afterwards, the counselor can ask:

- What are 2 things you learned about yourself during these sessions?
- What is something you learned about yourself that surprised you?
- What will you remember most about these sessions?

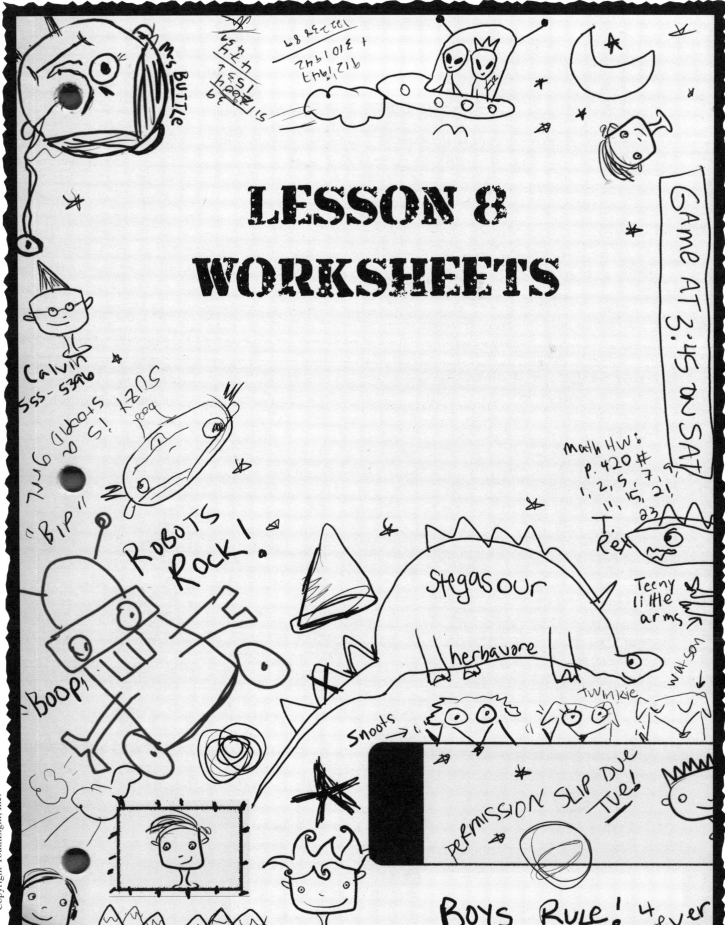

INITIATION AFFIRMATIONS

Complete one for each group member on a separate piece of paper. You can use this template or you can write your own affirmations.

Example:

Aaron, I want you to know how special you are to me and to the other members of this group.

I admire you because you: **are able to help others feel better when they are unhappy or hurt.**

I also like the way that you **use humor as a way to deal with tense situations. You are caring and loyal.**

Over the past 8 weeks, I have seen you **become more considerate of other's feelings.**

I know that you have the power to change the world in a positive way.

_____ , I want you to know how special you are to me and to the other members of this group.

I admire you because you:

I also like the way that you:

Over the past 8 weeks, I have seen you:

I know that you have the power to change the world in a positive way.

Reproducible Lesson 8

My Initiation Affirmation to You

_____

I want you to know how special you are to me and to the other members of this group.

I admire you because you

I also like the way that you

Over the past weeks, I have seen you

I know that you have the power to change the world in a positive way.

Good Luck!

_____   ____/____/20____

INITIATION SECRET #1

*"I light this candle to honor my brothers and to reveal the first secret of our group **(light your candle)**. Our Latin motto Amicitia, fortitudo et pertinacia, means friendship, courage, and determination. We have become friends over the last eight weeks. When we tried new experiences and shared our personal thoughts and feelings, we proved that we are courageous. We have shown determination in the fact that we completed all our lessons and stand here today, together, as a true brotherhood."*

Initiation Secret #2

*"I light this candle to honor my brothers and to reveal the second secret of our group **(light your candle)**. This is the secret meaning of the lion on our crest. The lion has a sun for a mane. The lion stands for leadership, strength, courage, honor, and loyalty. The sun represents knowledge and warmth. Together they are a shining symbol of what a real man can be."*

Initiation Secret #3

*"I light this candle to honor my brothers and to reveal the third secret of our group **(light your candle)**. The lines on the sides of the crest represent wings. When we follow our hearts and are true to ourselves, we can soar to great heights."*

Reproducible Lesson 8

INITIATION SECRET #4

*"I light this candle to honor my brothers and to reveal the fourth secret of our group (**light your candle**). This is the secret meaning of the hand on our crest. The lower left corner of the crest has a hand. The open palm symbolizes that we are always open to friendship with new people, even if they are different from ourselves. The open palm is also a secret group sign. If you see one of your brothers from this group flash you his open palm, you will know that he needs your help immediately. This way you can quickly come to the aid of your friends."*

INITIATION SECRET #5

*"I light this candle to honor my brothers and to reveal the fifth secret of our group **(light your candle)**. This is the secret meaning of the ship on our crest. The ship is heading east. East represents new experiences and new horizons. The ship is a symbol of joy, happiness, and adventure. Thus, this part of the crest reminds us that life is waiting to be lived and explored."*

Initiation Secret #6

*"I light this candle to honor my brothers and to reveal the sixth secret of our group **(light your candle)**. This is the secret meaning of the heart on our crest. It reminds us to follow our hearts. We should listen to our feelings and make choices based on what we believe is right for us. Brothers, I bid you remember – know thyself."*

INITIATION SECRET #7

*"I light this candle to honor my brothers and to reveal the seventh secret of our group **(light your candle)**. On the bottom left swirl of the crest lies a line and three dots. This is the Japanese symbol for mind, heart, and spirit. We now know that no one can be a real man unless they honor each of these areas in their life."*

INITIATION SECRET #8

"I light this candle to honor my brothers and to reveal the eighth and final secret of our group (light your candle). On the bottom right hand side of our crest is a turning spiral. When we do a good deed, it sets a spiral of change in motion. Your good deed prompts someone else to do a good deed," and so on until our one action creates a spiral of good for all those around us. Brothers, I encourage you to be the kind of person who starts many, many, spirals in life."

THIS CERTIFIES THAT

_____

HAS COMPLETED THE OPERATION BREAKING
THE BOY CODE PROGRAM AND HAS BEEN INITIATED
INTO THE BROTHERHOOD.

_____

Boy Code Brotherhood

Year: _____

Names from right to left:

References

Adler, P.A., Kless, S.J., Adler, P. (1992). Socialization to gender roles: Popularity among elementary school boys and girls. *Sociology of Education*, 65(3), 169-187.

Allen, D. (n.d.) *Your Sword in the Stone.* Retrieved August 30, 2008, from http://www.joydancer.com/circle_fire/swordstone.html

American Psychological Association. (1997). *Cartoons still stereotype gender roles: Males portrayed as doctors and scientists, females as nurses and bathing beauties.* Washington, DC: Author.

Franklin, C. (1984). *The changing definition of masculinity.* New York: Plenum.

Herr, N. (2007). *Television and health: Television statistics.* Retrieved September 10, 2008, from the California State University at Northridge Web site: http://www.csun.edu/science/health/docs/tv&health.html.

Hill, P. (1997). *Coming of Age: African American Male Rites-of-Passage.* Chicago, IL: African American Images.

Hill, P. (2008). *Harvesting new generations: Afrocentric rites of passage.* Retrieved October 10, 2008, from The National Rites of Passage Institute Web site: http://www.ritesofpassage.org/df99-articles/harvest.htm

Kindlon, D. & Thompson, M. (2000). *Raising Cain: Protecting the emotional life of boys.* New York: Ballantine Books.

Martino, W. & Meyenn, B. (Eds.). (2001). *What about the boys? Issues of masculinity in schools.* New York: Open University Press.

Media Awareness Network. (2008). *Common stereotypes of men in media.* Retrieved September 10, 2008, from Media Awareness Network Web site: http://www.media-awareness.ca/english/issues/stereotyping/men_and_masculinity/masculinity_stereotypes.cfm.

Pollack, W. (1999). *Real boys: Rescuing our sons from the myths of manhood.* New York: Owl Books.

Town, C. (2004). The most blatant of all our American myths: Masculinity, male bonding, and the wilderness in Sinclair Lewis' mantrap. *The Journal of Men's Studies,* 12(3), 193-205.

UNIFEM. (2001). *Masculinity and gender-based violence.* Retrieved August 30, 2008 from the UNIFEM East and Southeast Asia Regional Office Web site: http://www.unifem-eseasia.org/resources/factsheets/Gendis5.htm